STEWART PAYNE

CUT FROM THE CLOTH OF FOGO

STEWART PAYNE

CUT FROM THE CLOTH OF FOGO

A LIFE OF TEACHING, TRAVEL, AND MINISTRY

FLANKER PRESS LIMITED
ST. JOHN'S

Library and Archives Canada Cataloguing in Publication

Payne, Stewart, 1932-, author
Cut from the cloth of Fogo : a life of teaching, travel, and ministry / Stewart Payne.

Issued in print and electronic formats.
ISBN 978-1-77117-409-1 (paperback).--ISBN 978-1-77117-410-7 (epub).--
ISBN 978-1-77117-411-4 (kindle).--ISBN 978-1-77117-412-1 (pdf)

1. Payne, Stewart, 1932-. 2. Church of England in Canada--Newfoundland and Labrador--Clergy--Biography. 3. Newfoundland and Labrador--Church history--20th century. 4. Newfoundland and Labrador--Social conditions--20th century. 5. Newfoundland and Labrador--Biography. I. Title.

BX5620.P39A3 2015 283.092 C2015-903426-4
C2015-903427-2

PRINTED IN CANADA

RECYCLED Paper made from recycled material FSC www.fsc.org FSC® C103567

This paper has been certified to meet the environmental and social standards of the Forest Stewardship Council® (FSC®) and comes from responsibly managed forests, and verified recycled sources.

Cover Design by Graham Blair

Flanker Press Ltd.
PO Box 2522, Station C
St. John's, NL
Canada

TELEPHONE: (709) 739-4477 FAX: (709) 739-4420 TOLL-FREE: 1-866-739-4420
WWW.FLANKERPRESS.COM

9 8 7 6 5 4 3 2

Canada Canada Council for the Arts Conseil des Arts du Canada Newfoundland Labrador

We acknowledge the financial support of the Government of Canada through the Canada Book Fund (CBF) and the Government of Newfoundland and Labrador, Department of Tourism, Culture and Recreation for our publishing activities. We acknowledge the support of the Canada Council for the Arts, which last year invested $153 million to bring the arts to Canadians throughout the country. *Nous remercions le Conseil des arts du Canada de son soutien. L'an dernier, le Conseil a investi 153 millions de dollars pour mettre de l'art dans la vie des Canadiennes et des Canadiens de tout le pays.*

TABLE OF CONTENTS

PREFACE

I was born at home in Fogo, Newfoundland, in 1932, the tenth of eleven children born to Albert and Hilda Mae (Oake) Payne. Only six of the eleven children survived early childhood. My father died at the age of forty-eight when I was three years of age.

My story is made up of a number of short stories of events that happened to me growing up on Fogo Island and along the way, which have moulded and nurtured my physical and spiritual growth. I trust it will help people—young people in particular—setting out on life's journey, and like me at the starting point, face what might appear to be insurmountable obstacles and setbacks. In my life, I did have to overcome a number of obstacles but found that I could achieve my goals in those areas my God-given talents fitted me for, to contribute to the common good. I believe that everyone can make a difference, and my advice is never give up. The old cliché is true: where there's a will there's a way. Today, opportunities and possibilities abound more than ever before. The only failure is the lack of confidence in yourself to reach your goal. Work hard, search for opportunities, and find the help you deserve.

I share my story also because I am deeply, deeply grateful for all that I have been given along the way: for the blessings of family and friends, an education, and the opportunities to serve, to the best of my abilities, in the corporate life of the church and outside. Because of that, I am a thankful person.

Another goal is to pay tribute to my parents, Albert and Hilda Payne, my wife, Selma, and others whom I mention briefly but who nevertheless inspired and supported me all the way.

DEDICATION

My father and mother, Albert and Hilda Mae (Oake) Payne, my five siblings who died so very young—Arthur James, Violet, Gladys, Stanley, and Elsie Jean—my four siblings who lived full lives and died well into their eighties—Minnie (Hart), Cyril, Lewis Herbert, and Beatrice Brinson—and my one remaining sister, Mabel LeDrew.

A special thank you to Eileen Churchill, Canon Frank Cluett, Bishop Percy Coffin, Foster Lamswood, Canon Joyce Payne, June Pearce, the Rev. Dr. Alexander Daley, and the Rev. Hubert Coombs, who read my very first draft and encouraged me to keep on writing. I am deeply grateful to Elizabeth Scammell-Reynolds and Donovan Downer, my co-editors, for their patient critiquing of my text and for offering helpful comments and suggestions. I am grateful, too, to George Lee and Gordon Slade, who offered encouragement after reading a later draft. Finally, I am indebted to Rex Brown, who did the final reading and helped me organize the material. I would also like to thank the staff of Flanker Press.

Under different circumstances, my wife, Selma, would have been very understanding and supportive of my time and efforts in writing as she was throughout our lives together; my love and thanks to Selma. As you read this, you will understand that late in life she developed dementia and had no comprehension that I was writing this.

Thanks to Hilda Simms of Happy Valley–Goose Bay for finding a few special photographs for me. Thank you to our daughter Angela, who answered my many calls regarding issues with the computer. I take total responsibility for the content of the book, and I feel blessed with all the help along the way.

FOREWORD

I saw Stewart Payne for the first time in 1950, when I was seven and in grade two, and he was eighteen. Stewart had come to Indian Islands to teach. He arrived, as did all our teachers, in late August, and was boarded at Uncle Malachi Sheppard's house, a short distance up the road.

When we knew the teacher had arrived, there was much excitement in the small community. Soon, school would begin.

I knew Stewart was different. Besides his impressive height and sonorous but gently commanding voice, he had presence. His personality filled a room. As a shy kid at the time, I did not understand exactly what for, but I knew this man was destined for a much larger role. Stewart departed at the end of the school year, leaving us with great memories of a good teacher, along with the many interesting "things" he had taught us in our one, crowded, multi-graded classroom. For example, at Christmastime, Stewart thought the school should be decorated. He proceeded to show us how to fold brightly coloured crepe paper into alternating, overlapping squares. When he stapled the ends of the two rolls and let them drop, they opened out into some of the most beautiful decorations we had ever seen. Hung from opposite corners of the spacious classroom, these decorations received their full complement of "oohs" and "ahs" throughout the festive season.

My next contact with Stewart Payne came several decades later. The occasion was on a Saturday in July at Corner Brook, when Dave

Sheppard, who was on a visit with his family at the time. He and I had both been in Stewart's classroom at Indian Islands. We were walking past the bishop's house at Cobb Lane. As we approached the large two-storey house, we realized Stewart was out watering flowers and that he was now the bishop. We walked up the driveway, where he greeted me friendly, and then to Dave he said, "Hello, David Sheppard, how are you?" This a prodigious feat of memory from many decades before, and it illustrated that Stewart Payne was a man who loved people and that he remembered them, irrespective of how much time had passed. He was clearly a man of the people.

Stewart had a productive but short career as a teacher, over three years: at Wild Cove, Indian Islands, and Fogo. Even during his years as a member of the clergy, however, I believe he also considered himself a teacher.

Stewart spent full and busy years as a member of the clergy at Happy Valley, Labrador, his first charge, where he also served Rigolet, North West River, and Mud Lake, becoming inculcated into the Labrador way of life. He then served the Parish of Bay Roberts in Conception Bay, and later in the Mission/Parish of St. Anthony. He went on to become bishop of Western Newfoundland in 1978. In 1990, he became metropolitan in the Ecclesiastical Province of Canada. In 1986, Stewart was runner-up to Archbishop Michael Peers, who was elected primate of the Anglican Church of Canada. These were busy years in which Stewart contributed to the full in all he did, travelling extensively, while Selma stayed home and took care of the growing family.

This autobiography is a sensitive amalgam of the personal and of the professional. It is a great tribute to Stewart's wife, Selma, and their family and the love they all share. It is also a window into the many wonderful relationships he forged, with all the people he served as their pastoral leader over several decades, and some of the frustrations he had to overcome.

Reading his manuscript has been a great pleasure for me. It brought back vivid memories of a respected teacher and a person whom I call a good friend. I wish him well as he shoulders his great personal burden in the coming years as chief caregiver for Selma in her illness. My wish for him is that he finds peace and solace in the fact that he has served his family and the people well.

Don Downer
January 2012

CHAPTER ONE
GROWING UP IN FOGO, FOGO ISLAND

There were a number of places and communities on Fogo Island: Fogo, which included the areas of Lock's Cove and Eastern Tickle; Joe Batt's Arm–Barr'd Islands; Lion's Den; Shoal Bay; Tilting Harbour; Stagg Harbour; Seldom-Come-By, made up of Little Seldom, Wild Cove, and Bullocks Cove; Deep Bay; Payne's Harbour; and Island Harbour. Each was a world unto itself. There was very little instant communication between them. Because the livyers' livelihood depended on the harvest of the sea, connections by road were not developed. Generally, communities were isolated except by sea and trails. Where roads did exist, the work was done by hand, with pick and shovel. There was no heavy equipment like front-end loaders, graders, and heavy-duty trucks. To my knowledge, Mr. Thomas Butler, a tinsmith in Fogo, owned the first car on Fogo Island. That car was a spectacle to behold. We stood well back, in amazement, when that car came our way over the narrow dirt road.

Catching, salting, and drying codfish was the one and only industry, the backbone of the island's economy. The fisherfolk traded with the fish merchants in Fogo, Joe Batt's Arm, and Barr'd Islands, or with the Fisherman's Trading Union Company in Seldom-Come-By.

By the time I was born, Paynes had inhabited Fogo for over 200 years, starting with Nicholas and Elizabeth Payne coming from Poole, England. My father and mother, Albert and Hilda Payne, were the parents of eleven children born between 1913 and 1935. I was the tenth child, born at home June 6, 1932, and baptized by the Reverend Nathaniel Stewart Noel, our rector at that time, as Sidney Stewart. Four of the eleven—Arthur James, the first-born; Violet, the third; Gladys, the fifth; and Stanley, the sixth—all died within the first or second year of their lives, some years before I came along.

Elsie Jean, the last child, was born April 28, 1935, and was a little more than a month old when Dad died in June of 1935. Elsie Jean died on Christmas Eve, 1937, two years and nine months old.

The business of funeral parlours was not established on Fogo Island at that time. Preparations for the burial of the dead were done voluntarily by friends and neighbours. Visitation and reception took place at the home of the deceased. Nightly vigils known as wakes were held, leading up to the day of burial. On the day of the funeral, a mourners list was read aloud at the home, as family and friends lined up behind a horse-drawn hearse and proceeded to the church on foot for the funeral service. From the church the congregation walked behind the hearse to the cemetery.

The unshakable belief at that time was that God was the supreme, austere being up above, and everything that happened was according to the will of God. He operated on the basis of a plan of reward and punishment—reward for being good and punishment for being bad. When people died, it was said that their time had come, regardless of circumstances. God had taken them home. They were better off.

As humans grow in years, we grow in our perceptions of God and in our beliefs and faith. I now believe that our great mysterious God is love. I believe that when we die we go to God from whence we came, and, metaphorically speaking, into the arms of God's loving embrace. Home indeed. I do not believe that God had a purpose for me and only some of my siblings. In the mind of God there is a purpose for all people. That purpose is that we should journey in the awareness of love and service of God and neighbour. In the case of my five brothers and sisters who died very young, that purpose was thwarted by malnutrition, infectious and communicable diseases, like mumps, measles, whooping cough, and the lack of medical services.

Left: Cyril, Lewis, Mabel, Mother, and me with a puppy in my arms
Right: My father (with banner) during a funeral procession

The area on the north side of Fogo where I grew up. Our house is over the roof of the stage.

I don't think anyone can imagine the tragic loss and suffering our mother endured, losing five of her little children and her young husband, unless one has been through similar loss and suffering oneself. Even when Dad and Elsie Jean died, I was too young to understand what Mother was going through. My recollection is that she never opened up much to talk about her loss and hurt. She always seemed strong and resilient and got on with the business of the day, showing little of the sorrow and grief within. In the 1930s, the Depression years, life was hard for a lot of people in Newfoundland and Labrador. Our family was not alone in the toll taken by untimely deaths. In particular, the infant mortality rate was very high.

In those hard times there was a stoic faith summed up in the expression "God will provide." I do not doubt that God does provide enough to meet the needs of the world, but the truth is, resources are not managed properly and shared equitably.

Dad was an inshore fisherman and a cooper. Among his fishing gear were cod nets and trawls. He owned a rowboat (punt) in which he used a sail when the wind co-operated. He made only a meagre living for his family in the salt cod industry. He also harvested herring, caplin, seals, and seabirds in season, for the family table. Dried caplin was part of the winter food supply for the dogs and a pig. A few choice dried caplin were also set aside for the family table. Some years we had a sheep and a pig to kill in the fall, other years just one or the other.

Dad's fishing property included a stage and two flakes. The stages that dotted the shoreline of Fogo harbour came in all shapes and sizes. Dad's stage, extending out over the water, was a rectangular-shaped building approximately thirty feet long and twenty feet wide, with a peaked roof. On the water end of the stage was a wooden platform the width of the stage and extending about eight feet over the water. It had a wide ladder extending from the stagehead to the rocky harbour bottom. Here is where the boat tied up to off-load the catch and was the platform that accessed the stage from the boat. The stage was where the fish was processed for salting. There were fish pounds in the stage where the fish lay in salt for a week or two. Fishing gear and supplies were stored in the stage as well. On the shoreline near the stage was a structure made of logs called a cradle, which was used for manually hauling a boat out of the water.

His flakes, one on either side of the entrance to the stage and several feet off the ground, were wooden platforms used for drying the fish. The structure was made of fairly heavy, long, tapered poles, three or four inches in diameter, with the bark removed. We call them longers, or in the local parlance, "lungers." The longers were covered with a layer of fir or spruce boughs. This allowed the air to circulate from below and aid in the drying process.

The quantity of codfish caught was a seasonal gamble, and the quality of the finished product depended on the weather and the way the fish was handled. Because the merchants didn't know what the market fish prices would be until the fish was sold in the fall, the fisherfolk were never told what price they could expect. Everyone talked about the fish merchants as if they fleeced the fishermen. But it seems to me that the merchants also took great risks. They fitted out the fishermen in the spring of the year so that they had the basic food and fishery supplies, so they could prosecute the fishery all summer long. I expect that predicting the overseas market prices months in advance was a tricky business. The fishermen brought their dried salt cod to the merchant who had supplied them in the spring, and only then, if the catch was reasonably good and fish markets strong, did the merchant get paid for the outfitting. There were no unions, so fishermen seemed to be at the mercy of the merchants. In the case of a poor voyage, the merchant was the loser as well, and yet was expected to advance more credit next spring. Whatever was left over after the merchant was paid went on a note, and purchases were made against that note, a kind of barter system, or more formally known as the truck system.

There was very little cash in circulation. A child given a few pennies thought it was a fortune. On a stick of Beaver tobacco there was a small tin tag worth a cent or two. When I saw a man cutting up tobacco to fill his pipe or cutting off a "chew," I would ask if I could have the tag. Sometimes he would give it to me without my asking for it. Likewise, in the bottom of some paint cans, not that we saw a lot of paint, there was a metal tag worth a cent or two. As children we would vie with one another for those tags, because when taken to the store they could be bartered for a few common candies.

During the winter months, Dad made casks in his cooper shop near the house for one of the local merchants, Earle Sons and Company. The casks were used for packaging the dried salt codfish for export to foreign markets. The company supplied the lumber and Dad supplied the labour. For some years after Dad's death, my brothers Cyril and Lewis continued the business of making fish casks for Earle Sons and Company. I was older then but wasn't much help to them, although on occasion they would conscript me to bring materials into the cooper shop and have me use a handsaw to even off the ends of the staves. Once, when I was reluctantly doing that, and seeing my friends at play, I accidentally nearly sawed off the top off my left thumb. With the thumb bandaged, I was able to join my friends at play.

We lived very much from hand to mouth, as the saying goes, and close to the earth. We had a couple of small gardens in which we grew vegetables for our own use. We stored the winter supply of vegetables in a cellar underneath the cooper shop. We kept a couple of sheep that provided wool to be spun and made into mittens, socks, and sweaters. I can see now, in my mind's eye, the spinning wheel in the middle of the kitchen and Mom spinning wool into yarn. If it wasn't the spinning wheel that impeded access to the table, it was the mat frame. Every winter, Mom would hook two or three mats of colourful floral or geometrical designs. The coarser mat that was placed by the outside door for wiping boots was called a "raggy jacket."

We knew nothing about refrigeration, simply because we had little that required refrigeration. There was fresh fish: cod and salmon, which went straight from the water into the cooking pot. For the winter, there was salt fish, pickled herring, and pickled salmon. Any fresh meat, like pork or mutton, was procured late in the autumn when frost was in the air and there was no chance of spoilage. Seabirds late in the autumn and seal meat in March and April needed no refrigeration. If we bought a bottle of milk from someone who had a cow, it was used up long before it could spoil. Miracle Whip and Carnation milk were not on our shopping list. When Earle Sons and Company started up a fresh fish canning factory, they would pay men to haul large blocks of freshwater ice, which were stored in sawdust in a large warehouse and later used to ice down the fresh fish awaiting the cooking and canning process. Some individuals may also have kept an icebox. Pieces of ice from an iceberg put in the water barrel was a summer treat.

Except for a few people, like merchants, who had their own power generators, there was no electricity in any of our homes. Therefore, we were without indoor amenities like running water, bathroom facilities, and central heating. Television and telephones were unheard of. In time, some people acquired battery radios that were used rather sparingly, mainly for the Gerald S. Doyle news bulletin and popular songs.

Our only source of heat, summer and winter, was the kitchen cast iron stove—ours was the Ideal Cook model—which burned wood all the time, along with a little coal in the winter. As a result, all indoor activities took place in the kitchen. We lived in the kitchen. The small inside room—called the parlour, by some people—was used very little, usually as a mortuary room. Even in the winter nights, the fire in the kitchen stove had to be entirely extinguished and all vents and openings completely closed. Sometimes, to make sure the fire was out, Mom would pour water on the lingering embers. It was a nightly ritual to wind up the clock and put the cat outside, and when Lewis was home he would cut some chobies to light the fire in the morning. A choby is a piece of kindling with shavings carved on the side. After some years we graduated to a kitchen range with a warming closet on top and a water tank to one side of the oven, in which water was heated whenever the stove was lit. This water tank was one very early sign of modernity creeping into our homes.

On a frosty winter's morning, when it was reported that the kitchen was warming up, I would hop out of the warm featherbed, grab my clothes, run to the side of the stove, and get dressed. The water barrel, in the inside porch, froze over every night in the winter. We would break the ice to get some water, and we dared not waste any.

After a quick wash we were ready to eat breakfast. To make toast we took a fork and held a slice of bread at the grating in the front part of the stove, where the red-hot embers were.

We always tried to keep a few hens. The hens were rarely penned up in the summer but let out into the wide-open spaces. To prevent them from getting in the gardens and rooting out the seeds, we used a piece of cloth material to attach a foot-long birch stick, called a span, to the hens' wing joints on the back. The hens, especially the little chicks, were more like pets. They were never forced-fed to produce eggs all year round. In fact, they didn't produce any eggs in the winter. When they were outside in the spring and summer, there were occasions when we had to hunt for an egg because certain hens would lay their eggs outside and away from the henhouse. Collecting eggs was fun. If a dog got loose, a hen could be in trouble. Several times when someone forgot to bar the henhouse door at night, a dog got in and killed the hens. That's why I say that we were always *trying* to keep a few hens.

There were a couple of horses in our neighbourhood, but practically every family in the area kept a few dogs, used mainly for hauling firewood in the winter. Skidoos were unheard of. Our neighbours, who were mailmen, had many dogs. They hauled the mail by dog team every couple of weeks in the winter, from Port Albert in Notre Dame Bay to Fogo Island. This was a long, difficult, and at times hazardous trip through the country and over bay ice. The coastal boats (steamers) brought freight and mail in the summer.

My father died in June of 1935 at the age of forty-eight years, leaving mother at the age of forty years with seven children: Minnie aged twenty-one, Cyril aged seventeen, Lewis aged thirteen, Beatrice aged ten, Mabel aged six, myself aged three, and Elsie Jean aged one month. What I understand about father's death is not from memory but what I was told.

In the spring of 1935, while the ice was still around Fogo Harbour, he was helping a neighbour, Thomas Simms, build a wharf. All the work was done by hand and the workers were often cold and wet, handling logs in and near the water. One of the logs Father was putting in place rolled and struck his leg, skinning out the shin bone. At the same time, a supply ship came in to the edge of the harbour ice and Father, with several other men, helped unload the much-needed supplies using a sled on the ice and a punt (rowboat) in swatches of open water. He came home Saturday evening cold, wet, and feeling unwell. He had supper and went straight to bed. The following Tuesday, he died. Mother was certain that his death was caused by an infection in his leg, which spread poison throughout his body—simple blood poisoning. Dr. McKenzie was on the island that year and he was contacted. He sent over some pills that had little effect. Better medical services were simply not available.

I have only a few vague recollections of my father. I seem to remember him sitting at the end of the kitchen table with Mabel on one knee and me on the other. Again at the kitchen table one mealtime, Mother was choking on something she ate and Dad rushed to her relief. I have a misty picture of him walking up the path to our house. My final recollection of him is when someone lifted me up to see him in his casket.

With very few cameras around, the only family pictures we had were taken by my Aunt Phoebe (Oake) McKay from Boston, after Dad's time. After many inquiries and searches, I finally found a single small picture of Dad as one of six pallbearers at a funeral. As soon as I saw the photograph, I recognized him as the one who must be my father. The facial resemblance to his brother, my uncle Walter Payne, and my brothers Cyril, Lewis, and me, was clear. I extracted his photo from the group picture, had it enlarged, and gave a copy to each of our family members. Enlarging it from a very small print doesn't make for a very clear photograph, but it appears here.

With Dad not there anymore, there was not much fishing from our immediate waterfront. I got myself into trouble a few times, because on calm, sunny, summer afternoons with nothing to do and nowhere to go, I would sneak down to the stage, untie the punt, and row around in the harbour in the immediate area of our property until spotted and summoned ashore. Understandably, Mother and my sisters were a bit overprotective of the youngest little rascal, especially around the waterfront alone or with boys of his own age.

When I was older, I went out to the fishing grounds with a neighbour a few times to jig a codfish, help haul a trawl, or to watch men haul a cod trap, but I had no inclination to stick with it. Seasickness was a deterrent, though one could overcome that if one persisted. I did enjoy being in someone else's fishing stage, putting fish on the splitting table, cutting throats, heading fish, cutting out cod tongues, and getting all wet and slubby in the bargain. Neighbouring fishermen shared with us whatever produce from the sea they had at the time.

I was often instructed, as I hung around a fishing stage, "Here, take that fish up to your mother," or, "Would your mother like to have a fish?" or, "Come on, cut out some cod tongues for your mother."

In the mid-1930s on Fogo Island, there was very little that a woman could do to earn money, apart from domestic work and making fish. Once a year, for a very small wage, Mom, with other women, scrubbed Earle Sons and Company's store. She also did housecleaning for a few families, for which she was often paid in kind, and made fish.

Part of the salt cod fishing industry involved schooners with their crews, from the Island of Newfoundland, going each spring to the fishing grounds along the coast of Labrador. Some had accommodations on shore and brought the fish back to their stages for processing. Others lived on board their schooners all summer, prosecuted the fishery from there, and returned home in the late summer or early fall laden with hundreds of quintals of salt bulk codfish in the holds of the schooners.

Captain Patrick Miller, with a crew from Fogo, was involved in the Labrador fishery summer after summer. On returning home he would distribute the salt bulk codfish to whoever was able and willing to make the fish for him. Captain Miller or one of his men would come around in a motorboat to see what Mother could do. She would agree to take fifteen or twenty quintals at a time, a quintal being 112 pounds. Then a day or so later, the motorboat would return with the fish. Men standing in the boat would yaffle the fish—stack several fish on top of one another—and throw it up to men on the stagehead. It was then passed from one to another and neatly stacked in a pile in the stage.

Next came the making of fish. A puncheon tub, made from sawing a molasses cask in two, was set up in the stage, waist high, and partially filled with salt water drawn up from underneath the stage or over the stagehead. Several fish at a time were placed in the tub of water. Mother and whoever was around to help her—one of the older children or a neighbour—dressed in long rubber boots and wearing aprons made out of flour sack material dipped in linseed oil to make them water resistant, began the process. Each fish was washed clean by hand and placed in a pile on the stage floor. This fish so washed was referred to as waterhorse fish because of the process of washing in the water and spreading it on a flake, a frame (horse), to dry. When the washing was complete, the fish, several at a time, were placed on a hand barrow—a flat, rectangular wooden frame with elongated handles at each end for two people to carry—carried out on the flake, and spread out to dry. In late afternoon or evening, the fish was gathered into small piles called faggots and covered with whatever was at hand—rind (tree bark), large tubs, pieces of canvas—or little houses made for that purpose. Mother worked hard making fish, but we all chipped in as we were able, and commanded to help. Neighbours often gave a hand. We stored the fish in the cooper shop.

The Hart family picking up fish

When the fish was well dried, the owner, Captain Patrick Miller, or his men, came by in motorboat, collected the fish, and took it for sale to one of the fish merchants. The sale of fish was referred to as shipping the fish. For all the hard work, Mom would get fifty cents a quintal.

As well as helping with the making of fish, the family members all helped making hay for the sheep, sawing and splitting firewood, bringing water from our own well, feeding the animals and hens, and tending the gardens. When I came home from school I heard again and again the familiar words, "Take off your bit of good clothes, your school clothes, and put on those old overalls and bring in the wood and water." Meanwhile, being the youngest, I was spared some of the hardships and heartaches my older siblings endured around the time of Dad's death.

Widows received a small quarterly government allowance often referred to as the widow's mite. At first Mom used to receive $15 a quarter. When my two older brothers, Cyril and Lewis, began earning a little money, the welfare officer came round to inform her that she would now be cut back to $10 a quarter. I remember that incident very well because I knew the hurt it caused. In the fall, when Earle Sons and Company was packing dried salt cod for export, she would get several weeks of work there. When the company started up the fresh fish canning factory, she worked there summer after summer, adjusting the weight of fish in each can before it was capped and sealed. I am quite sure that by this time she ceased to receive the widow's mite. Through it all, in those Depression years, we didn't have to receive the government's welfare of seven cents a day, referred to as the dole.

My three sisters went out "in service" in Fogo. In service meant doing housework for a family, taking meals with the family, and being paid five or ten dollars a month. In some cases the worker lived with the family. Minnie was already working with Mrs. Dina Payne when Dad died. She later married Bertrum Hart and they raised a family in Fogo.

Beatie went in service with Mr. and Mrs. Harold Earle and later married Harvey Brinson. They raised a family on Change Islands and later moved to Lewisporte.

Mabel went in service with Mr. and Mrs. Brian Earle until she married Claude Barnes and they raised a family in Fogo. Mabel's second husband, Hayward LeDrew, died in 2015. Mabel now lives in a retirement home in Grand Falls–Windsor.

Cyril became a permanent employee with Earle Sons and Company in Fogo as manager of the fresh fish canning factory, and as a cooper in the off-season. He married Edna Bennett and they raised a family in Fogo. Edna is now in a long term care home in Clarenville.

Lewis became a fisherman for many years as a shareman with another fishing crew. He worked with Cyril in the cooper shop some winters and later worked as a seaman on vessels operated by Earle Sons and Company. Lewis married Ruby Hart and raised a family in Fogo. The pay that Lewis received as a shareman depended on the quantity of fish caught and on the agreed system of shares. From the time he shipped on with a fishing crew in May, often referred to as "going in collar," he lived with them as one of the family and did whatever work there was to be done around the place. When it came to fishing, the man who owned the boat and fishing gear, who also lodged and fed the hired men, took a number of shares. The hired men got a share of what was left. The hired men were thus called sharemen.

Besides the challenge of working hard to maintain the family and keep us all together, Mother was a self-taught midwife. She attended the birth of practically all the children born in our area on the north side of Fogo. Whenever the call came, quite often late at night or in the wee hours of the morning, she would rise and go. Because there were no telephones in those days, the call would come as a knock on the side of the house underneath her bedroom window. "Hilda, so-and-so is sick, can you come right away?" She attended, usually with another midwife, but would do the follow-up care for days and days afterwards, with no thought of receiving anything for it. She was also available to care for the sick. I recall a time when she worked all day in the fish factory and stayed up three nights in a row with Mrs. Primmer, a terminally ill neighbour. She must have caught a nap now and then. She was gifted, strong, and determined, all for family and others in need.

Our sports and play were very simple and unorganized. The

games we played were hide-and-seek, rounders, much like softball only the ball we used was often a rag ball, and football on the harbour ice, with a pig's bladder for a football. When someone killed a pig, the bladder was already bargained for. After a week or two in pickle it was blown up by mouth and served well as a football. We rolled barrel hoops around on the road, pretending they were bicycles, and sailed our small homemade boats wherever we could find a source of water, sometimes in the landwash.

My first pair of skates was an old pair that I discovered in the loft of our old store, the ones that screwed on the heel of a boot with a strap over the front part. I thought I had a fortune when I found them, but they kept coming off and damaging my boots in the bargain. In the end I had to discard them. There were no organized hockey games. In winter we entertained ourselves sliding on our backsides on whatever we could find to sit on. We made snow houses and snowmen, had snowball fights, and hung out with friends.

In the spring of the year, with the harbour ice melting and breaking up along the shoreline, there would be several loose pans of ice on which we would jump and run, from one pan to another. This was called ranking or copying. It held its dangers as well as its excitement. We always ended up soaking wet and falling into the water. Then came the hardest part—having to go home in fear of punishment, mindful that we had been warned not to go on the ice. A bit later in the spring, we spent time making and trying to fly our kites.

In summer, when we were free from work chores, we tried to swim in the cold salt water off the stagehead or in a small swimming hole inland in a place called Frenchmens' Well. In the landwash we looked under rocks for crabs and from the stagehead we fished for tomcods and sculpins.

In summer we picked blackberries and herts—low-bush blueberries—on the hills on the north side of Fogo. We feasted on those and sometimes brought a few home to share and for use in a pie or pudding. Most summers there was a bumper crop of blueberries and partridgeberries in over the hills on the south side of Fogo and around the centre of the island.

When the berries were ripe, several of the neighbours, usually women and children, made their plans for a day trip. A blowy day, no good for fishing, brought some of the men into the plans as well. We would cross the harbour in boat and walk in over the hills with buckets, flour sacks, empers—an emper was a smaller container in which we picked the berries and emptied them into the larger container—and lunch bags in hand. The hills came alive with the sound of cheers and laughter as we hastened to find the best spots of berries. As we came upon the native fruit, the cry went up, "Lots of berries over here," "Come over here," "Don't tread on the berries," and, "I almost got my emper full already."

Conversations went on about the berries, the heat, the fact that the flies were eating someone, and parents warning children to stick to their spot and pick only ripe berries with no dirt among them. We didn't always make time for a boil-up but welcomed the break for a lunch of tinned beans, bread, water, and tea. As day drew to a close, tiredness or boredom would settle in for some and the conversation would turn. "When are we going out? We have enough berries now, let's go home." Soon afterwards, with buckets and bags sufficiently full, we contentedly made our way home.

In my teenage years, I didn't sit around idle all summer. When fish was being shipped to Earle Sons and Company, I would hang around their wharf with my peers, anxiously awaiting the word from the wharf foreman, Joseph Snow, to get down into a boat and yaffle up the fish. When vessels docked, laden with coal or salt, we were also there, making our presence felt and indicating our readiness to work. At the end of the day we would gather around Mr. Snow as he recorded the hours worked, or put down our time, as we used to say. When cooperage for the making of fish casks was being delivered at our place, there was a sure job helping to unload and carry the materials to their storage place. The maximum pay we ever received for those casual jobs was ten cents an hour. It afforded Mother a few more dollars with which to purchase an item of clothing and some school supplies for the coming September.

Christmas was a very special time, much anticipated and long awaited. Christmas didn't really begin until we had been to church to mark and celebrate the birth of the Christ Child. We never expected a lot by way of presents. Even a few simple things were appreciated. An apple and some candy in my stocking were special. Presents were practical things like scribblers, exercise books, pencils, or a pencil case, and a doll for a girl, a cap gun for a boy, or a mouth organ. Scribblers were for day work in school using a lead pencil, while exercise books had finer paper and were used for homework using pen and ink. A child didn't get all those things at any one Christmas, but these were the sorts of things that made for presents at Christmastime. One Christmas, Mabel and I were given a homemade slide each for going downhill over snow or ice and for pulling one another around. Cyril had made them and painted them red and green in different designs, to distinguish Mabel's from mine. They weren't as fast as the factory-made slides that some of our friends had, with metal frame and runners, but they were special and made us very happy.

One Christmas I remember very vividly. Lewis had been fishing all summer as a shareman with Mr. Fred Leyte and crew. The fish were not too plentiful that summer, so he ended up having little money to show for all his hard work. In the fall, he went off to Cox's Cove in the Bay of Islands to work in the herring factory. However, out in the cooper shop, he had left a few large salted codfish, partly dried. It might have been my idea that if those fish were dried enough we could sell them and have a little bit more money to spend on Christmas fare. The week before Christmas, one night, past the time for visitors, I carried the fish into the kitchen and hung them up by the tails on a line over the kitchen stove to harden them up. The next day I shipped (sold) them to Earle Sons and Company. I have no idea how much money I received for the fish, but it did make a difference in what we could have for Christmas.

Mummering, or jannying, was a carnival affair that lasted from December 26 to January 6. We had no proper costumes or masks and limited costume materials. We borrowed from one another, turned garments inside out, and stuffed pillows inside our clothing. A mask or "false face" was made by cutting holes for the eyes and mouth in a piece of cloth and draping it over the face. Disguising our identity as much as possible, we called at the homes of friends and neighbours, asking in a muffled voice, "Any mummers 'lowed in?" There was always a greeting and a warm welcome. If someone had an accordion, a mouth organ, or a Jew's harp, he or she was encouraged to play, and we danced around the kitchen. If there was no musical instrument, someone might be persuaded to play the comb or the spoons. Playing the comb was performed by putting a thin piece of paper over the comb and humming a jig in a muffled voice. The spoons were clapped together in rhythm. The hostess would offer some refreshments such as a drink of syrup or some other sweet-flavoured juice called clingy.

All the while, the guessing game went on. "I know who this is but I'm not going to tell." Being so tall and lanky, about which I was always self-conscious and sensitive and often teased, even with a couple of pillows stuffed inside my clothing, I was always the first one identified. When they knew who we were, we would lift back our false faces and have a good laugh. On we would go to the next house and do the same all over again. There had to be a very good reason to turn away mummers. Sometimes more than one group arrived at a house at the same time and the house would be full. The more the merrier. When we were not out mummering, we stayed at home and welcomed all who came to the door.

Our family was more or less typical of families in the neighbourhood and throughout the community. We were close. The hard times in the 1930s and 1940s that we faced together brought us closer to one another. Our love and concern for one another was not always verbalized or demonstrated with kisses and hugs, but it was very real just the same. Mother taught us to say our prayers and to say grace at every meal and from time to time gathered us around her to hear the Bible being read.

CHAPTER TWO
CHURCH

Church was a big part of my upbringing. All of my family, from an early age, went to St. Andrew's Church morning and evening most Sundays, and to Sunday school in the afternoon September to June.

In Fogo we actually had a separate Sunday school building, used strictly for Sunday school, the Meek Memorial Building, which stood in memory of the Reverend Christopher Meek, one-time rector of the Parish of Fogo. We were graded by age, girls in their classes on one side of the building, and boys in their classes on the opposite side of the building. Much was made of memorization. Older students stood before the teacher and recited the collect of the day, a short liturgical prayer appropriated to each Sunday, special days and seasons, and used right before the Scripture readings in the Holy Eucharist service and at morning and evening prayer. Sometimes an older student recited a part of the catechism, a series of instructions using questions and answers found in the Book of Common

St. Andrew's Church, Fogo

Prayer, or recited a portion of the Gospel reading for the day. Each year we advanced from one class to the next. At the conclusion of each year, prizes were given, taking into account attendance and how well we had learned our lessons. The superintendent of Sunday school in my time was Arthur Earle. The male teachers who taught me were Thomas Loder, Wilson Jones, and William Sibley.

The highlight of the year was the summer Sunday school picnic. The sign that the picnic was going ahead was the church flag at topmast. It was an exciting time. We each brought a cup or mug from home to hold any beverages. Mothers attended with the smaller children and provided sandwiches and cookies for tea time. Quite a few of us would meet at the Meek Memorial Building and parade to the picnic grounds, about a mile away, behind some of the houses on the south side of Fogo, to a spot "in the country," chanting and waving small flags, in all probability the Union Jack.

Throughout the afternoon there were a number of competitive activities, class races, sack races, three-legged races, skipping, and tug of war, in which winners received prizes. There were candy scrabbles for girls in one area and for boys in another area. For a candy scrabble, we would all gather round and a teacher would throw candy out among us, for which we all scrabbled to get as many candies as possible, usually ending with many of us collecting scrapes and bruises along with the goodies. Later in the afternoon we sat around on the ground and tea was served. A couple of men had boiled the water over an outdoor fire and made the tea. I can hear the teachers and older students now as they came around with large kettles of tea, calling as they came, "Tea, milk, and sugar, tea, milk, and no sugar, tea, sugar, and no milk." Sandwiches and cookies came next. After the tea there were more of the same activities. At sundown we helped clean up and put things away for another year. Tired but happy, we gathered up our loot and wended our way home.

Some observances of the church year, Lent for example, made an impact on all of us. In my growing up the common question leading up to Ash Wednesday, the first day of Lent, was, "What are you giving up for Lent?" We didn't have a lot of extras, whether plain or luxury items.

I remember giving up sugar in my tea one Lent and candy another Lent. The idea of self-denial or fasting in this penitential season was to remind ourselves of what Jesus gave up for us, for our sins—His life on the Cross. The money saved through giving something up was given to the church as a Lenten self-denial offering and went in support of some special project. Nowadays we tend to think not so much about giving up something we particularly like but rather trying to break a bad habit and or taking something up by way of love and service to others.

Some of the commandments, the fourth for example, had a big influence. "Remember that thou keep holy the Sabbath day" was well observed. Not all were regular churchgoers, but almost every resident of Fogo refrained from unnecessary work on Sundays. It was a rare sight to see anyone go out to haul a cod net, trawl, or cod trap on a Sunday, except if their fishing gear was at risk of damage from storm or a stray iceberg. The only time anyone would spread a few fish on a Sunday was if it had been raining all week and the fish, under cover, was deteriorating. Apart from church and Sunday school, there was little that we were allowed to do on Sunday except go for a walk or visit someone.

Ash Wednesday morning, the whole school, teachers and pupils, paraded to St. Andrew's Church for a worship service. Lenten services were held every Wednesday and Friday night in Lent. We were allowed out those nights but strictly to go to church and come right home afterwards.

Good Friday was a day of solemn prayer and fasting. By way of a fast, we were not allowed to have butter on our toast Good Friday morning. It was some sort of fish for the rest of the day. If you liked fish, it was not much of a fast. I don't know how the tradition came about, but it was a practice not to throw water outdoors on Good Friday. If you did, it was as if you were throwing it in the Lord's face. A great part of the day was spent in church, especially for the three-hours watch at the foot of the Cross, from noon to 3:00 p.m. At first I didn't look forward to spending three hours in church, but I was always amazed as to how quickly it seemed to pass. What made a big difference was that I was there together with my friends and family.

Easter, as we celebrated the resurrection of Our Lord, was a joyous occasion. The worship services were very upbeat, with choir processions, loud with alleluias. It was a custom for girls to have new Easter bonnets and the boys to have something new, too—new shoes or perhaps a new suit of clothes. A new suit of clothes could well be a hand-me-down or one made over.

The Diocese of Newfoundland had a "Home and Foreign Mission Fund." In support of this fund, the diocese supplied parishes with small wooden missionary boxes. They were given out, at least one to a family, and throughout the year children in the family took it upon themselves to deposit as many pennies as possible in the box. Toward the end of the year a special missionary service was held in St. Andrew's, attended by many parishioners and some clergy from the neighbouring parishes of Joe Batt's Arm, Barr'd Islands, and Change Islands. There would be a guest preacher as well. At that service, children brought in their missionary boxes and, at the time of offertory, proudly carried them up and placed them on the altar. It was a moving service as we heard of and thought about people far away who would now, as a result of our offering, be able to have a missionary bringing the Gospel to them.

We saw the bishop briefly, once in four or five years, because he covered the whole of Newfoundland and Labrador and most of it by sea. The confirmation preparation classes, Bishop Abraham's visit, the actual confirmation and Holy Communion, all coming at the same time, held such anticipated promise and euphoria that immediately afterwards there seemed to be a letdown. Following my confirmation on July 10, 1944, there was a period that summer when, like many others, I got away from going to church. For me the absence from church didn't last long because our rector, the Reverend Isaac Butler, followed up and invited several of us to join the choir. We were quite excited about the prospect. It was a big deal, to dress in a black cassock and a white surplice, put out the hymn boards, light the candles, and carry the processional Cross, all in addition to singing in the choir with the adults.

The Church Lads' Brigade (CLB) played a significant part in my growing up. We met Saturday nights, September to June, in the hall belonging to the Society of United Fishermen. We each made the Church Lads' Brigade Promise, part of which says, "I will try to be clean in thought, word, and deed and be a Christian gentleman." We learned through drill and physical exercises the importance of taking and obeying orders, good posture, and self-discipline. We paraded publicly, in uniform, and attended church together, as a company, on special occasions.

Walking home from the CLB in the winter nights always caused me some concern. On the last three-quarters of a mile I was alone, and in that area several households had dogs that were not tied up in the winter. There were rumours that there were a few saucy dogs among them. The stillness of the frosty night would be broken only by my footsteps, which in turn alerted some of the dogs, causing them to bark and run in my direction. I was never attacked by a dog, but I was mighty glad, those Saturday nights, when I reached the latch of our porch door.

CHAPTER THREE
SCHOOLS

There were three schools in Fogo: an Anglican school, a United Church school, and a Roman Catholic school. There was very little communication among the three institutions, except for a spirit of competition among students as they passed, going in opposite directions to their own schools. This spirit sometimes erupted in a snowball fight or an actual fisticuff affair. Each one felt that his or her school was the best.

St. Andrew's School in Fogo was simply three fairly large classrooms, a pot-bellied stove in the centre of each classroom surrounded by rows of student desks. The original desks had iron frames with wooden seats and tops and accommodated two students in each one. The single desk and chair came a bit later. There were very little resources except a blackboard and chalk, an abacus, which was a reckoning table with sliding beads, a globe, a few maps, and prescribed textbooks. There was no electricity, running water, or indoor toilet facilities. Outhouses were the order of the day, one for boys and one for girls. Without a gymnasium, there was nothing by way of a physical education program or organized sports. There was no music program. We improvised our own games. We played tag, rounders—a sort-of softball—chased one another around, and made our own fun. In the last couple of years of my schooling, the old St. Andrew's School was replaced by a new four-classroom building, now a senior citizens' home. The only difference in any of the schools on

Fogo Island was the size of the buildings and the number of multi-grade classrooms, depending on the student population.

There were no janitorial services. The older girls swept the floors and emptied the trash cans two or three times a week. Two or three times a year the mothers were asked to come with scrubbing buckets and utensils to scrub the school—wooden floors, desks—throughout. The older boys, in grades seven to eleven, took weekly turns lighting fires in the pot-belly stoves each morning and tending them throughout the day.

The old St. Andrew's School, Fogo. I attended there for seven years until the new school was built.

It was long before the days of school buses. We walked to and from school twice a day. In the winter, if a storm blew in while we were in school, the menfolk would be there in the school porch with scarves and extra clothing to bundle up the children and walk them home for the rest of the day.

A hand bell was rung from the school bridge—the platform at the school entrance we called a bridge—by the principal or designate, to call us in for the start of the school day. The morning classes started at 9:30 a.m. and ran until 12:30 p.m. The afternoon session was from 2:00 p.m. to 4:00 p.m. and ended with prayers and, in some cases, a Scripture reading. At a morning assembly of the whole school, we sang a hymn and said prayers. When there was no music, I was one of several who might be called upon to rise (start) the hymn. Religious education courses were given as well.

I still hold the position that we had good, well-qualified teachers. Their positive attitudes and care seemed to bring out the best in their students. I was an average student, never at the top of the class. I had to work for what I got. I liked school and during what seemed like the long, idle summer couldn't wait for classes to begin. In high school I enjoyed the mathematical subjects—arithmetic, algebra, and geometry—more than the reading subjects. School wasn't compulsory in those days. With parents' consent a student could leave school for some sort of employment, as did my older siblings. The dropout rate was significant. There was the attitude that a boy didn't need an education to be a fisherman and a girl didn't need an education to be a housewife.

I'm sure I misbehaved as often as some others, but I only got the strap once, in grade seven, several times on both hands. This form of punishment is no longer allowed in our schools. A strap was a strip of real leather, a portion of a leather belt, perhaps. In the teacher's eyes I deserved what he gave me for turning around and talking to the person behind me.

The teachers I remember are Rita (Simms) Harnett, Clara (Noble) Earle, Edith Ludlow, Blanche (Durdle) George, Norman Batten, Stanley King, Harry Adey, and Arthur Young. They all made a lasting impression on me. The two that stand out most are Stanley King, my grade nine teacher, and Arthur Young, my grade eleven teacher, because those were critical years marking the beginning of high school and graduation from high school. There were no graduation exercises. When we received the public examination results in August and found out that we passed, that was all there was to graduation exercises.

Practising for and staging the annual Christmas concert was a highlight of the school year. The rooms and halls were appropriately decorated for Christmas, including a manger scene and a beautifully dressed Christmas tree. The student body took part, singing Christmas carols and folk songs, reciting verses, re-enacting a scene from the Biblical Christmas story, and performing a few short dialogues and skits. The excitement was high when Santa arrived and distributed gifts to all from underneath the tree.

We carried a snack to school for recess time. There were no cafeterias or breakfast programs, but for a time the Department of Education supplied all schools with cod-liver oil and cocoa malt. The teacher would distribute the cod-liver oil for use at home. In some cases the teacher would prepare and serve the cocoa malt at recess time. The bigger boys would take turns fetching a large kettle of water from a nearby well. By recess time the kettle would be boiling and the cocoa malt ready to serve. We all stood in line with our mugs to get our share. There were occasions when a teacher would distribute the cocoa malt among the children for use at home.

This incident about the cocoa malt being served in school stands out in my mind. One morning while the teacher, Miss Edith Ludlow, was stirring the cocoa malt, her hanky fell from her sleeve into the kettle. We can laugh at it now, but it wasn't so funny then because we couldn't have any cocoa malt that day.

A lot of vocations to ordained ministry come through the church community, young people being involved all the way through. My call certainly came through St. Andrew's Church in Fogo. Over the years there have been a goodly number of clergypersons from Fogo Island. I knew those who were studying for ordination at Queen's College in St. John's. I heard their stories when they returned home from college, and I saw the direction in which they were going. That had a profound effect on me and my decision to become ordained. I was very much an average lad growing up, like other boys in the neighbourhood and at school, but people would say to me again and again, "I know what you are going to be when you grow up. You are going to be a minister." It made me think. Did they know something that I didn't know?

The prophet Isaiah, in the Book by the same name, tells how in the temple he had a very significant experience and heard his call: "Whom shall I send and who will go for us?" And he answered, "Here am I, send me." Those words have always had much meaning for me. They are indelibly etched in my mind and heart. St. Andrew's Day, November 30 each year, I heard the hymn, "Jesus calls us, o'er the tumult, of our life's wild restless sea, day by day His sweet voice soundeth, saying, Christian follow me." One of my favourites, it has had great meaning for me, too.

The call comes to people in different ways. We know from Holy Scripture and our tradition that God calls ordinary people from inconspicuous places to be leaders in the church and in the world. I have never seen a vision or heard a voice, as such, but God has spoken to me many times and in many places, through the words and examples of people, like those words of the prophet Isaiah and the St. Andrew's Day hymn.

My schooling was a blessing. Being the youngest sibling, I was afforded the opportunity to stay in school whereas the older ones had to quit school and find work to support themselves and the family. I was the only child in the family who had the opportunity to complete grade eleven. Dad had no formal education. He couldn't read or write. Mother always said he was determined, that his children would get an education, even if he had to sell his shirt to make it happen. I hope he knows that we all did our best, according to the opportunities before us, to fulfill his dreams for us.

CHAPTER FOUR
FOGO BOY OFF TO ST. JOHN'S

Nineteen forty-nine was the year that Newfoundland and Labrador became part of the Canadian Confederation. Without a radio in the house, the only news was second-hand from folks in the neighbourhood, and that was often slanted according to an individual's preference and political ideas. We heard a lot about how much better off we would be if we became the tenth province of Canada. The social benefits of family allowance, old-age pensions, and unemployment insurance were hugely attractive. On the other hand, there was the unfortunate suspicion that all that would come at too great a cost, that we would lose ownership of our properties, as well as our identity and culture as Newfoundlanders. I was too young to vote and too old to receive family allowance. Life after high school, with its many challenges, caught my attention a good deal more than governmental affairs at the time.

In 1949, my final year at St. Andrew's School in Riverhead, Fogo, I had to give some thought to life after grade eleven. Ministry was always on my mind, but the time and process to get there was not immediately clear. I was sure that I was too young and lacked the resources to explore that path right away.

There were very few salaried job opportunities open to high school graduates on Fogo Island and few other options except fishing, teaching, or the ordained ministry. The route that others had followed to ordained ministry was to teach for a few years before pursuing studies for ordination. There are lots of parallels between teaching and pastoral ministry; a priest is always a teacher. I felt certain that I would enjoy teaching.

From the 1949 graduating class in St. Andrew's School, five of us—Faith Willis, Willa Hart, Frank Reid, Rex Leyte, and I—decided that we would like to go to the six-week summer school at Memorial University College in St. John's and begin teaching in September. The principal of St. Andrew's School was Arthur Young, a very fine person, an experienced teacher, and a great principal for whom we had the greatest respect. We didn't ever think to call our teachers by their first name, even if we knew it. It was always "Miss" and "Mr."

Mr. Young encouraged us and helped us complete the application for summer school. It was a great day when we received the news that we were all accepted. Rex Leyte had made an inquiry and informed me that his uncle and aunt, Mr. and Mrs. Harold (Sadie) Simms in St. John's, were prepared to have him and me stay with them for the six-week period. Everything was a go, or was it?

The easy part for me was getting accepted and finding a boarding house in St. John's for the six-week summer school program. Where would the money come from to outfit me and cover all the other associated costs? More than once I feared that it might be impossible, that it might be a step too big for me to take. Was it fair to expect the family, with such limited resources, to deny themselves for my benefit? Would I be asking too much of them?

From time to time Mother assured me that she would make it possible for me to go to summer school if that was what I wanted to do. She enlisted whatever help Beatie and Mabel could contribute, and together they fitted me out with clothing, a new suit, new shoes, shirts, and ties. It was a very special moment, a tearful, joyous moment never to be forgotten, when Mother handed me all the hard-earned money she had sacrificed to save, totalling $50. Lewis followed at the same time and gave me the only money he had, $50, which he had earned from salvaging cargo and equipment from a wreck at sea. I felt so fortunate, so blessed and grateful for the outfitting and the money, and deeply appreciative for the love and generosity from which it all flowed. Used very sparingly, the $100 would have to cover all expenses for the six weeks of summer school, including travel, tuition, school supplies, and accommodations. There would be very few incidentals or treats.

Apart from the coastal steamers, the mode of transportation from Fogo Island was by passenger boat to Lewisporte, Notre Dame Bay. There were other passenger boats from time to time, but the *Fogo Flyer* out of Joe Batt's Arm, owned and operated by Harvey Cobb, made two or three scheduled weekly trips from Fogo Island to Lewisporte. From there it would be the Canadian National Railway train, the "Newfie Bullet," to St. John's.

The boat in this picture, the MV *Miami*, owned and operated by Fred Chaffey on the Lewisporte run, was similar to the *Fogo Flyer*.

I can see the *Fogo Flyer* now, steaming up through Fogo harbour one morning in early July, stopping to pick up passengers at the Newfoundland and Labrador Export Company wharf, at Earle Sons and Company wharf, and at the canal. The canal is a narrow channel running from Fogo harbour to the sea beyond. It was covered by a concrete bridge. With suitcase in hand I joined the *Fogo Flyer* with other passengers at Earle Sons and Company wharf. The proper send-off had taken place privately at home, with all the appropriate advice about being careful and all the dos and don'ts. As the *Fogo Flyer* pulled away from the wharf, I waved goodbye to family and friends standing on the wharf. Faith, Willa, Frank, and Rex would join us at the canal. I was on my way to a whole new world.

I hadn't been off Fogo Island before, so this would be a brand new experience. The six-hour trip from Fogo to Lewisporte was very pleasant. The weather was fine. We sat out on deck and enjoyed the scenery and one another's company. The *Fogo Flyer*'s second hand, Don Decker, was entertaining and kind to us. When lunchtime rolled around he served us bully beef—canned corned beef, likely from Australia—mustard pickles, and store-bought bread. It had to be the best thing going at that time. I think about our trips on the *Fogo Flyer* every time I see a can of corned beef.

As the *Fogo Flyer* neared the dock in Lewisporte at around 3:00 p.m., we gathered up our belongings and prepared to disembark. Willa Hart had a sister and brother-in-law, Muriel and Robert Randell, who had relocated to Lewisporte from Fogo some years before, and we could go there until about 10:30 or 11:00 p.m., when it would be time to catch the branch train to Notre Dame Junction. We thanked Harvey Cobb and Don Decker for a great trip and made our way to the train station, my very first taxi ride. After checking in our luggage at the train station, we enjoyed the friendly, kind hospitality of the Randell family. Janet Randell, sister to Robert Randell and who became a long-time friend, was living with them. It was good to reconnect with Janet again. At about ten thirty we boarded the branch train, which took us in to Notre Dame Junction.

At about midnight, at the junction, we could hear the train rumbling down the track. The clickety-clack grew louder and louder as the bright headlight came into view. The train slowed to a stop at the station. This was the time of year when a lot of people were travelling. School was out and people were on the move. The train, I could see, was packed full of passengers, and in my innocence about such travel I figured that a lot of those people would disembark here, making room for us. A few people did get off, and as others started to board I realized what was happening. This was just another stop along the route from Port aux Basques to St. John's. We climbed aboard with everyone else, but every seat was taken and many were left standing. The girls eventually found seats, but several of us lads had to stand, or sit on our suitcases through most of the night. I did manage to squeeze into a seat from time to time, but only momentarily before giving it up to a woman and child at the next train stop. Seven or eight hours later we arrived in St. John's. Rex Leyte's uncle Harold met us at the train station and took us to his home on Pennywell Road. During the first week in St. John's my head kept spinning because of the constant motion on the train.

As I reflect upon those days, I wonder how we kept in touch with our folks at home. There were no telephones in Fogo and certainly none of the modern-day technological communication gadgets. The only means of contact at my disposal was through a telegram or letter. I can believe that I sent a few letters home that summer. There is a common saying, "No news is good news." If folks at home didn't hear from us right away they figured everything was all right.

As I see young people today with all the modern-day communication gadgets, texting their families and friends and keeping in touch continually, I am amazed at all the changes that have come about. I trust we won't move too far from the personal and social contacts with one another. I have a computer, and a simple cellphone that is more for emergency use than anything else.

In St. John's, I had indeed entered another new world, a world where there were cars galore, paved streets, tall buildings, telephones, electricity, indoor plumbing, and running water. Rex and I walked from 296 Pennywell Road to Memorial College campus on Parade Street. For the first week it was easy enough to find our way down to the college, but coming back was a puzzle. We found it difficult to find the street that led into Pennywell Road. After a while it became quite straightforward.

The college on Parade Street was not big and complex compared to the Memorial University of Newfoundland and Labrador campus of today, but compared to St. Andrew's School in Fogo it was awesome. There were multiple classrooms, all numbered, the lecture theatre, a large common room, a marvellous library, and something I had never heard talk of before—a gymnasium—and so much more within those hallowed halls of learning.

Registration and orientation took some time. There were no familiar faces among the students or professors, so we had to get to know one another and make new relationships. There was a different professor for each of the five or six courses we were taking. The professor came into the classroom at the sound of the bell. When the bell went again, the forty-five- or fifty-minute lecture was over. There was a short break before we were into another lecture with a different professor. It was all so novel, exciting, and challenging. There was no organized sports program and very little activity in the gym. Not having a proper gym outfit and no knowledge of basketball and volleyball, I shied away from the gym. We were encouraged to use the library to do research for assignment papers. I did that in my free time. There was one field trip during the summer—buses took us all to Bowring Park one afternoon. Saturdays, which were free, afforded us the opportunity to see something of St. John's. Mr. Simms kindly showed us around. It was a big adjustment to make. It was awesome, too good to be true. We were teachers in the making. Some people I got to know that summer were Nelson LeGrow, Nathan Kettle, Walter Cull, Evelyn Shiwak, and Wallace House. Our paths would cross again at another summer school, at university, and in the workaday world.

Our boarding mistress, Mrs. Simms, was very kind and caring but strict. Even in those days, long ago, she would not tolerate smoking indoors. Even Mr. Simms would repair to the back garden to smoke his pipe. We soon learned, too, that we were expected to keep to our upstairs room for study and not litter her parlour with books and papers.

We went to the Cathedral Church of St. John the Baptist every Sunday morning with Mr. Simms. I was awestruck the first time entering this large stone cathedral of Gothic design and architecture.

There was so much to see and question that it was hard to concentrate on the worship.

Mrs. Simms packed a picnic basket practically every week, and the four of us were off to Bowring Park on Sunday afternoons. It was such a treat to check out places of interest in the park. As the afternoon wore on, Rex and I were starved. We could hardly wait for Mrs. Simms to spread a cloth on the ground and open up the basket of goodies.

One evening, Mr. Simms took Rex and me to Buckmaster's Field to see a wrestling match. I had never seen anything like it before. I felt scared to the point of being sick at the sight of all those spectators aiding, abetting, and watching two men beating up on one another. I was glad when we walked away from there but afraid, too, that we might be held responsible as accomplices. How naive I was!

At the end of the six weeks, we each had an interview with our respective denominational superintendent of education, with the prospect of being sent out to teach in September. Our Anglican superintendent at that time was Mr. R. L. Andrews. His office was behind the old Newfoundland Hotel. There was a shortage of teachers in those years, so during the interview Mr. Andrews offered me three possibilities: Nipper's Harbour, Round Harbour, or the sole-charge school in Wild Cove, Seldom-Come-By, on Fogo Island. I knew nothing about the other places and little about Wild Cove, except that we had relatives there. I was yet hesitant to venture too far afield, so I accepted the sole-charge school in Wild Cove. The superintendent would inform the school board that they had a teacher for Wild Cove beginning in September.

It was taken for granted in those days that all Anglican male teachers would automatically become lay readers in the church, to lead morning and evening prayer. In some cases a lay reader had to do a burial in the absence of a clergyman. At the end of the 1949 summer school we assembled at the chapel in Queen's College on Forest Road, and each one received a lay reader's licence under the signature of the diocesan bishop, Bishop Philip Abraham. We did not receive any particular lay reader training. It was assumed that as teachers we would be capable of speaking and reading well in public.

Then, with a probationary teacher's licence and a lay reader's licence in hand, I went back home to Fogo to await with excitement the start of a teaching career. I remember, as the *Fogo Flyer* drew near Fogo Island, thinking how bleak and barren it was compared with St. John's and other places along the route with their many trees and abundant grass. But it was home sweet home. Within a few days I would be on my way to teach school in Wild Cove.

I went to summer school at Memorial University the following summer of 1950, as did Faith, Willa, and Frank. Rex, meanwhile, had gone to work with the Bank of Nova Scotia in Fogo. I had saved enough money from teaching in Wild Cove to see myself through summer school in 1950. The only change in our mode of transportation was from Lewisporte to Notre Dame junction. Instead of taking the branch train, we pooled our resources and took a taxi. The unpaved road was dry and very dusty. That summer of 1950, the four of us boarded with Harry and Dulcie Oake, originally from Fogo, who lived on LeMarchant Road in St. John's, opposite the Grace Hospital. I was now travel-wise, somewhat familiar with the city, the university campus, and the routine, which made for a more relaxed and easy time. The courses of instruction during the second summer were, as expected, a bit more advanced.

Every Sunday we dressed in our Sunday best and went to church, morning and evening. As we walked up and down LeMarchant Road on a Sunday evening, to and from church, we were surely spotted as those outport summer school students.

Harry Oake was a seagoing captain. One Sunday afternoon, July 23, 1950, he took Willa, Faith, Frank, and me with some of his family on board his boat in St. John's harbour out through the Narrows, to see the sinking of the *Eagle* off shore. The *Eagle*, a wooden ship which had been in service to the seal fishery for many years, was now to end her days at sea. She was proudly towed out of St. John's harbour with all her colours flying. When she reached the site of her burial, the floodgates were opened, flares were set off on board, and she slowly, slowly, went beneath the waves, with her colours the last to disappear. This marked the end of an era. We reflected on her long years of great service. It was sad to see the waves close over the last flag.

What was so important about both summer schools was that I was exposed to so much that was different from my upbringing. I saw something of the wider world, I grew in self-confidence, and I acquired the ability to be a team player. All that, in addition to some teaching skills that I acquired, prepared me very well to begin and enjoy teaching. After the 1950 summer school I went home to Fogo for a few days, and from there to Indian Islands, where I would teach for the school year 1950–51. I had already been accepted for that position.

CHAPTER FIVE
SCHOOLTEACHER AT WILD COVE, SELDOM-COME-BY

There were very few cars on Fogo Island in 1949. Ross Anthony owned a jeep and provided my transportation to Bullocks Cove in Seldom-Come-By. From Bullocks Cove to Wild Cove, about four to five miles away, there was a footpath over the hills and through swampy ground. I waited at Heber and Bessie Dawe's house until my cousins Bert and Herbert Harnett were finished the day's fishing and were ready to leave for home in Wild Cove, and could assist me with my belongings. Bullocks Cove was usually referred to as "up the harbour."

Wild Cove was just a small village, an indentation in the shoreline on Fogo Island, and wide open to the Atlantic Ocean. There was no protection from storms at sea. As soon as it was evident that a storm was brewing, with gale-force winds blowing onto the land, boats had to be driven around to safety in Bullocks Cove, where there was more shelter. Small boats (punts) had to be taken out of the water. All men were inshore fisherfolk or retired. There were thirteen families in Wild Cove, very much like one big family, dependent on and supportive of one another. After the demise of a few families and the departure of others to find employment, the time to resettle came in the mid-1950s, when the remaining few families moved up to Bullocks Cove. Some floated their houses around Burnt Point into Bullocks Cove. One or two families maintained their houses in Wild Cove as their getaway cabins. Wild Cove today looks very much like it did before it was settled.

The school house-chapel in Wild Cove

Left and right: Stewart, teacher in Wild Cove, 1949–1950

Herb and Bert, whose parents were Joseph and Priscilla Harnett—Priscilla was Mom's sister, affectionately known as Aunt Press—took me to their family home. The only other member of that family was a daughter, Dorothy, affectionately known as Dottie, who because of some limitations could never be on her own. Uncle Joe and Aunt Press lived next door to the little schoolhouse. Throughout the year I would visit them nearly every day because Aunt Press was so thoughtful, kind, and caring. I was as much at home with them as I was with the folks in my boarding house.

The boarding house for the school year was with an elderly couple, Uncle Bill and Aunt Emma Combden, distant relatives. They boarded me for $25 a month. They had none of the modern conveniences like electricity, indoor plumbing, or running water, not that I was used to those things at home anyway. As soon as I was settled in my boarding house I found a key to the school and went along to see what supplies had come in over the summer and what I would have to work with. The schoolhouse was small, with just two rows of seats, one on either side of a pot-belly wood stove in the centre, with the teacher's desk in the front of the classroom. I could see myself in the role of the teacher. The excitement was very high.

School opened on the first day of September, with an enrolment of thirteen pupils, beginners to grade eight. Some days we could have fourteen pupils depending on whether or not one young chap, Eric Eveleigh, who could neither hear nor speak, decided to join us. Eric, thirteen or fourteen years old, came and went at will. He liked to have a relationship with the teacher and pupils and had a desire to keep in touch. I learned a lot of the communicating signs that Eric used and we had a good understanding. When I tried to engage him in the work we were doing, he would soon get bored, get up, and leave. He liked to draw and was very good at that. If only he could have attended a specialized school, he would have done well. Out of school Eric was friendly, too, and often made contact.

All the adults and children were so respectful and appreciated having school in their own little community. I felt very much like one of them. I adapted well to the work of teaching. It was serious business but fun. There was very little to do beyond the school day except prepare for the next day's lessons and correct work the children had completed. To go for a walk and drop into someone's house for a visit was about all one could do. There was one house in particular in Wild Cove that the younger folk seemed to gravitate toward, Esau and Beatrice Eveleigh's home. Aunt Beat was a daughter of Uncle Bill Combden. She and Esau had no children of their own. They were so welcoming and affectionate toward all. The evening would not be complete without dropping in to see them. Being absent for a few evenings meant that you had to give an account of your absence when you went by again.

The rector of the Parish of Joe Batt's Arm cum Seldom-Come-By, the Reverend Joseph Ayris, lived in Joe Batt's Arm and visited Seldom on a monthly basis for worship. I'm pretty well sure that, except in the winter, he walked from Joe Batt's Arm to Seldom-Come-By on most of his visits. He was the person through whom I received my teacher's pay. Because of an accidental fall he was unable to make his regular visits and, as a result, I received my first paycheque sometime in November. The monthly wage was $63.

Although it was customary to use the school as a chapel when necessary, the folks in Wild Cove attended the Church of St. Augustine up in Bullocks Cove. When the rector was not there, Richard Dawe, who taught school in Bullocks Cove, and I took turns leading morning and evening prayer in St. Augustine's Church.

I made one brief visit home to Fogo at Christmastime that year. My mother and her sister Aunt Minnie Wooldridge walked across the island, wheeling my old bicycle, and made one short visit to Wild Cove that year. Lewis made a couple of brief visits on foot to Wild Cove while I was there.

During the course of that first winter I received a letter from the Reverend Tobias Short, rector of the Parish of Fogo, asking me if I would go to Indian Islands to teach the following year, 1950–1951, partly because they didn't have a lay reader at Indian Islands. I accepted the appointment.

Left: Eric Eveleigh in front of the school in Wild Cove
Right: Children in front of the school entrance in Wild Cove, Seldom-Come-By

Left: Uncle Bill Combden, with whom I boarded when I taught school in Wild Cove, Seldom-Come-By, 1949–1950. Right: Aunt Emma Combden, with whom I boarded when I taught school in Wild Cove, Seldom-Come-By, 1949–1950.

CHAPTER SIX
TEACHING ON INDIAN ISLANDS

Indian Islands, not all inhabited, are separated from Fogo Island by a stretch of water known as the Stag Harbour Run. Stag Harbour on Fogo Island was the nearest community to Indian Islands. The larger community and my school were on Eastern Indian Island. I boarded for $30 a month with a marvellous couple, Malachi and Emily Sheppard, and their daughter Phyllis. Electricity and running water hadn't yet come to Indian Islands, nor had telephones or television. They did have a battery radio that was used sparingly to listen to the news and the songs.

The school was a one-room building with forty-five pupils in all grades, beginners to grade eleven. The grade eleven student, Clarence Penney, came for the fall session, successfully wrote supplementary papers before Christmas, and went teaching in Eastern Tickle on Fogo Island in January. The grade ten student, Llewellyn Collins, came to school after the close of the fall fishery and left again to pursue the fishery in the spring without sitting for the public exams. The four grade nine students—Florella Collins, Vera Kinden, Fred Penny, and Yvonne Frampton—contributed much to school life, attended regularly, and helped with the lower grades. They passed the public exams with flying colours. All forty-five were good students. I found it frustrating trying to teach all subjects in all grades and not having the time to do justice to it. Fortunately, there was nothing by way of discipline problems. The days of one-room denominational schools are gone, thank goodness, but in those days it was a given in our small outport communities, and teachers took it all in stride, not knowing any better.

Our rector, the Reverend Tobias Short, was unable to make regular visits to Indian Islands that year due to health problems. In addition to school, Monday to Friday each week, I conducted Sunday services, morning and evening prayers, and Sunday school in the school classroom every Sunday afternoon. I did have help with Sunday school. Some of the young ladies in the community and some of my senior students became Sunday school teachers.

Schoolchildren on Indian Islands

I officiated at my first funeral on Indian Islands—babies born to Jethro and Frances Collins—twins who died soon after birth. Frances was the daughter of Malachi and Emily Sheppard, with whom I boarded. It was special—an honour—to be able to offer spiritual guidance to the grieving parents and relatives. Teachers, especially in insular and isolated places, served in many capacities and were held in high regard. I was always addressed not by name but as "Teacher" by so many in the community, even in my boarding house.

There wasn't much to do outside of school- and church-related activities, though both kept me fully occupied. I made friends with a number of young people around my own age. We walked wherever we went. Raymond Hynes and I would go up to Nathaniel Kinden's or Maxwell Boone's on alternate evenings for a game of flinch, a popular card game. There was no regular boat link between Fogo Island and Indian Islands, although if you knew that a motorboat was going to and from, you might catch a ride. Bad weather and slob ice in Stag Harbour Run made winter travel uncertain and sometimes dangerous. I would not take the chance of getting stuck on Fogo Island and miss school, so I stayed put on Indian Islands for the whole of the school year, September to June.

As far as I knew, the organ was the only musical instrument used in the church in those days. We had two organists at the Indian Islands church, Mrs. Florilla Kinden and Mrs. Effie Boone. Effie taught me the keyboard and assisted me in the practice of a few simple hymns. In any spare time I would go to the church alone and practise for hours on end.

ONE-ROOM SCHOOLS

One-room schools were fairly common in outport Newfoundland and Labrador in those days. The picture I give here is from my teaching in the one-room school in Wild Cove, Seldom-Come-By, on Fogo Island, in 1949–1950, and in the one-room school in Indian Islands, near Fogo Island, in 1950–1951.

Both communities were small, tightly knit, and rather isolated. The folk in those communities knew each other well. Many of them were related to one another by bloodlines or marriage and were dependent on one another. When the time came to take the boats out of the water for the winter, the call went out and a sufficient number of able-bodied men came together and gladly gave a hand, knowing that within hours they would need the same help. The same practice applied when the time came to launch the boats in spring of the year. When people saw a neighbour in need of any kind, the help was readily forthcoming. People visited with one another. It might be for a game of cards, a chat, or refreshments always referred to as a lunch.

In those sole-charge, one-room schools I taught all subjects in all grades. The school day began with prayer, followed by roll call and marking the attendance register. On hearing his or her name, each pupil responded by saying "present." There was no choice in subject areas studied, since the curriculum was entirely prescribed. All grades would be working on the same subject at the same time, either arithmetic, literature, spelling, history, or geography, but they might be at different grade levels. The only science was general science. Laboratories and libraries were non-existent. I did my best to teach the prescribed subjects, but the main emphasis had to be on the three R's: reading, writing, and arithmetic.

Homework was a given. Before the afternoon session ended, I made sure they all knew their homework assignments, sometimes writing it up on the blackboard. The next day I corrected any written homework, grade by grade, in turn. To check on their reading assignments in literature, history, or geography, I also took each grade in turn. I had the pupils stand by their desks, or in a straight line facing the front of my desk, and gave each one some practice in reading. It soon became evident whether or not they had done their homework. Following the reading they went to their seats and worked on certain questions relating to the chapter while I spent time with another class.

For spelling I also had the class stand in line, and I tested each pupil in turn. Spelling a word wrongly meant going to the end of the class line. As another person went to the end of the class line, the previous person worked his or her way toward the front again. Words misspelled had to be written out, to reinforce the learning before being tested again. While I was teaching a lesson to one class, all the others were assigned seat work.

Both schools were heated with a wood stove. The stove in the school on Indian Islands was a forty-five-gallon oil drum half-filled with rocks and ash. It was replaced with a proper wood stove before the cold winter weather really began. The families supplied the firewood. In some cases it required the children having to bring a few junks of wood each morning. The bigger boys took turns a week at a time lighting the fire an hour or so before school opened and keeping the fire going all day. The maintenance and cleaning of the building was the work of the fathers and mothers. The girls would sometimes sweep the floor, do the dusting, and wash the blackboard, but the mothers would scrub the school two or three times a year.

My high school class, St. Andrew's School, Fogo, 1951–1952

There were no serious behavioural or disciplinary problems. The parents and I had the same expectations of the children. The children knew that they could never play one off against the other. The penalty for being late for school, not doing homework, or misbehaving in school could be losing all or part of the recess period that day, or staying behind ten or fifteen minutes after class was dismissed to write lines related to the offence.

The only physical education the schools offered were some simple warm-up exercises on severely cold winter mornings while waiting for the classroom to heat up. Weather permitting, the children made their own fun and played outside during recess time or while waiting for school to begin. The only organized attempt at leadership training and healthy lifestyle was the Junior Red Cross (JRC). JRC meetings, led by more senior students, were held periodically. We all received a list of health rules reminding us to practise good hygiene, to cover coughs and sneezes, get ten to twelve hours of sleep at night, eat the right kinds of food, fight germs in every way possible, and get plenty of fresh air and exercise. We proudly wore our JRC lapel pins.

TEACHING AT ST. ANDREW'S SCHOOL IN FOGO

I spent the summer of 1951 at home in Fogo, working at Earle Sons and Company's store. My plan now was to go to Memorial University of Newfoundland (MUN) in St. John's in September and do a full year of teacher training and get a first-grade teaching licence. This would mean obtaining a student grant from MUN and teaching three more years in return, or repaying the money as if it had been a loan. Although everything was set to go, I had a nagging feeling all summer that, come September, I would find myself as principal of St. Andrew's School in Fogo.

The school board hadn't been successful in finding a principal. A few days before school was to open the board met again, and following the meeting that night, two board members, William Sibley and George Oake, came to me, as I expected they would, and asked me if I might delay my going to MUN and take on the job of principal of St. Andrew's school for a year. My answer was quick and in the affirmative because I had been imagining for some time what was going to happen. I sensed, too, that after another year of teaching I would be ready to go to MUN and Queen's Theological College, in September of 1952, to begin my studies for ordination, three years sooner than I would have, had my plan for further teacher training materialized. Could the hand of Providence been at work in all this?

The principalship of the school in Fogo was not an easy assignment for a young, nineteen-year-old lad who grew up in Fogo. In addition to being the principal, I had to teach all subjects in grades seven, eight, nine, ten, and eleven in my home classroom. I had just graduated from that school two years before. The students in grades nine, ten, and eleven had been students in the same classroom with me in 1949 when I graduated. I was one of them and it was difficult to distance myself and claim the authority of the position. On the whole they were great students, but the public examination results in grades ten and eleven were not as good as we would have liked. It was different from my two previous years, in one-classroom, sole-charge schools, in Wild Cove and Indian Islands.

In the course of the year I helped out in St. Andrew's Church as a choir member and as a lay reader. The rector at that time was the Reverend William Mercer and the long-standing lay reader was Mr. George Oake. After teaching for three years I managed to save $1,000, which is what I had as I began five years of study at MUN and Queen's College in preparation for ordination.

CHAPTER SEVEN
THEOLOGY STUDENT, QUEEN'S COLLEGE, 1952–1957

In answer to my letter asking to be admitted to Queen's College to study for ordination, I received the following reply from Canon J. A. Meaden, the principal.

> Queen's College
> St. John's
> Newfoundland
>
> Dear Mr. Payne,
>
> I have your application form, which will be laid before the Bishop, as soon as he returns from England. I feel I can say in advance that I shall be very glad to welcome you to the College.
>
> You might talk over with Mr. Mercer, the course of reading, between now and September, which will be most helpful. I should suggest doing some Latin as far as time will permit and the text of the Bible with the help of the New Commentary, which you might be able to borrow from Mr. Mercer. The more familiar you are with the text of the Bible the better. I quite appreciate your responsibility as principal of a large school in your own home. Your duty to the school must come first.
>
> With all good wishes,
> Yours faithfully,
> J. A. Meaden

PS. I will write you again as soon as I can consult the Bishop and the clergy whose names you have given. J. M.

Soon afterwards, a second letter came.

Dear Mr. Payne,

I am glad to be able to inform you that the Bishop has accepted your application for admission to the College in September. The College will reopen on September 18. This date is set by arrangement with Memorial University, which opens a little earlier for registration. I shall be away all the summer and will not return until about the 8th of September. Perhaps you might consult Mr. Mercer about a cassock and surplice, which you will need. He will be able to advise you. What time you have for study, give to Latin and English, these being two very important and difficult subjects.

Wishing you every blessing,
Yours faithfully,
J. A. Meaden, Principal

September 1952 witnessed my departure from Fogo to enter a new world of theological study and training. The old Queen's College on Forest Road in St. John's was a residential theological school founded by Bishop Spencer in 1841 and re-established by Bishop Feild in 1844. It had accommodation spaces for thirty to thirty-five single male students on the second and third floors and was equipped with a dining room, common room, lecture room, library, and a chapel on the ground floor. The principal, the Reverend Canon J. A. Meaden, and Mrs. Meaden lived in a residence attached to the college. The young women who did the college housekeeping, cooking, serving meals, and cleaning lived in the principal's quarters.

There was a long-standing model of theological education leading to ordination—that of young, single males. It was unheard of that a married man could seek ordination. It was strictly a residence with no accommodations for married men and their families. We were never told outright, but there seemed to be an expectation that a man had to wait two or three years after ordination before seeking the bishop's permission to marry. It happened in a few cases that a young man quit theological training, got married and pursued another profession or went directly into the workforce with some previous related training. The training and ordination of both men and women, single and married, came later, in the days of the new, non-residential Queen's College on the campus of Memorial University.

Fred Haines and Stewart Payne, new students in 1952

Fred Haines and I were the two new theological students to enter Queen's in September 1952. When the college wasn't filled with theological students, men in other faculties at MUN were accommodated according to available space. It was a new experience to be in an all-male residence as one big family. Mrs. Meaden was very much a mother figure.

I was assigned a room on the top floor in my first year. The only window in the room was a skylight, which admitted sunlight and could be opened to admit fresh air as well. The room was quite adequate, with a comfortable bed, a chest of drawers, a table, a chair, and a place to hang up clothes. Year by year we were assigned different rooms, going from the top floor in the first year to the second floor thereafter.

The teaching staff over the five years consisted of the principal, Canon J. A. Meaden, the vice-principal, the Reverend Allan Gibson for the first year or two, and then the Reverend Mark Genge, the tutor, the Reverend Canon Stanley Allen, and visiting lecturers from time to time: Dr. Miller, health matters; the Reverend Percy Hiscock, Christian education; and Mr. Bruce Feather, elocution. In my first two years I did other courses at MUN—English, history, Latin, Greek, etc.—as credits in the Bachelor of Arts program, and one General Bible course at Queen's. In the next three years, as well as doing some courses at MUN, I did more courses at Queen's—Hebrew Scriptures, New Testament Studies, church history, doctrine, liturgy and worship, and ethics. The general ordination exams were set and corrected in England. Some credits went toward the Bachelor of Arts (B.A.) degree at MUN, and all toward the Licentiate in Theology degree at Queen's.

Stewart, in the area of Bowring Park, St. John's, while a student of Queen's College

Formation of a healthy, personal spirituality was nurtured by regular, faithful attendance at the daily chapel services and a disciplined lifestyle that included a personal prayer life and meditation. Life at Queen's was governed by the bell. The bell told us when it was time to rise in the morning, around 7:00 a.m., when it was time for chapel, when it was mealtime, when it was time for study in our own individual rooms, when it was time for tea break in the common room, and when it was time to be in our own rooms and quiet for the night. The only footsteps heard after the curfew bell were usually those of the senior man making his rounds to ensure that the rules of the college were being obeyed.

There wasn't much by way of a formal sports program. We walked wherever we went, to and from MUN particularly. Some took to running in the early morning. Some played Ping-Pong in the college basement. Some of us played basketball in the RCMP gymnasium on Kenna's Hill Saturday afternoons, with David Pearce as our coach. I loved to play basketball and had the height for it, but I came to it too late in life to really excel. Being so tall, skinny, and sensitive whenever my team was asked to take off their shirts to distinguish us from the other team, I lost interest and had a hard time staying on the floor.

Every Sunday morning, all theological students sat in the choir at the Cathedral of St. John the Baptist whether we could sing or not. We were never asked to practise with the choir. I guess it was one way to ensure that we were all in church together and exposed to the liturgy being very well done, since the cathedral should and did set the pace in liturgy and worship, as in many other areas. It was a tradition that theological students would take turns walking from St. John's to Torbay, approximately five miles, for a Sunday afternoon service or teach the Sunday school Bible class at the cathedral parish hall. It was understood that you walked to Torbay and didn't accept a ride. For the first year I took my turn walking to Torbay, and after that I was assigned to the cathedral Bible class, which was a Sunday school class of young people in their teens.

Most of the students who stayed at Queen's College were from outside St. John's and had very few contacts outside Queen's and Memorial University. We were allowed some free time Wednesday, Saturday, and Sunday evenings but had to be back in the college by ten or ten-thirty. Saturday night we had to be robed and in the chapel at ten o'clock for worship.

I always felt so privileged and thankful to have the opportunity to attend university and Queen's College that I never allowed myself to take it for granted. More than once, toward the end of a term and in anticipation of the final exams, I would look at myself in the mirror and say, "You cannot afford to fail a course. Repeating is not an option." Nights when we were allowed out, I and others like me would stay in, catch up on some reading, finish an assignment, and socialize among ourselves. Along with that, of course, was the fact that to go out to a movie or other social engagement, alone or with a girlfriend, one had to have money. For me, this was a rare commodity. By the time bills and fees were paid, there was nothing left. For months on end there was no money. Care packages from home containing a few packages of cigarettes were much appreciated and shared around. When I could better afford to smoke, I gave it up.

It was fairly common practice for a student who came back to the college after curfew to alert the occupant of one of the rooms where the lights were still on by throwing a pebble up to the window. That student would then tiptoe downstairs, hoping not to encounter a member of the staff or the senior man in the meantime, and let the culprit in. A student caught coming in late was summoned to the principal's office the next morning.

Although a few students complained, I didn't find anything wrong with the food at Queen's College. We were served fish every Wednesday and Friday, and to some folks' taste the salt fish may not always have been the best in the world. In my first year, one Friday at noon, as the bell went for dinner—luncheon now—we filed into the dining room with the smell of salt fish in the air. The principal, Canon John Meaden, was absent. Some of the senior students had a plan and announced that we were not to eat the fish but put it back on a serving table in the corner of the dining room. We all followed our instructions, some rather reluctantly, and left the dining room. We didn't hear much about the incident afterwards, but we were later served the fish in the form of fish cakes and the leaders of the demonstration were put in their places.

One event we all looked forward to each year, after the pressure of Christmas exams and before going home for Christmas, was the Christmas party in the college library. The library was appropriately decorated and arranged with tables for two couples each lining the walls. Quite a few of our lady friends were nurses-in-training from the General Hospital or teachers-in-training from the Bishop Jones hostel. We used taped music for dancing, waltzing for the most part. The friendly spirit of ease, lightheartedness, joy, and Christmas was in the air as we enjoyed the company and fun.

The first year at MUN and Queen's College, there were many adjustments to make and study habits to acquire. I hadn't the opportunity to do much Latin in day school, which meant that I was a conditional student and had to do Latin A that first year, which was a composite of grades nine, ten, and eleven Latin. I failed Latin A by a few marks. Working in St. John's that summer of 1953, and having some spare time to study, I acquired the grade eleven Latin text and signed up to write the grade eleven Latin public exam. The result was that I obtained a very good mark, seventy-five per cent, which meant that I could go on to Latin One in September of 1953. When I went into the Latin One class in September, Mrs. Cochrane, the lecturer, gave me a puzzled look and said quietly, "Mr. Payne, you are not supposed to be in here." After I explained to her how I had completed grade eleven Latin in June, she smiled and said, "Well done, you can stay."

I can honestly say that I learned more English grammar in university days doing Latin than I ever did doing English, because to do translation correctly I had to brush up on English grammar. I did Latin One from Mrs. Cochrane and Latin Two from Professor J. B. Ashley. In retrospect, it would have been to my advantage later on had I done some French courses, but it is important to see, too, the advantages of doing the prescribed Latin courses.

Five consecutive years at MUN and Queen's College would have been impossible without the love, care, and support of many people, number one among them my mother. I always felt that she would have been happier if her youngest son had found something to do in Fogo and be at home with her, yet she sacrificed and gave everything she could to ensure that I had what I needed to pursue my call, and dream, and complete the program of preparation for ordination. All of my siblings, with limited means, were as supportive and helpful as they could be. Parishioners of St. Andrew's Church in Fogo were also very supportive. Mrs. Flora Furze, who operated a small general store in Fogo and came to St. John's from time to time, always contacted the principal of Queen's in person to find out how her Fogo boys, Frank Reid and Stewart Payne, were doing. After her visit with the college principal, he would inform me, "Your good friend from Fogo was here this morning to see me." I always knew who that good friend was. Each year just before Christmas a cheque would arrive from Mrs. Furze, just enough for passage money to go home for Christmas and back to Queen's again. We had to vacate the college for Christmas so that cleaning and maintenance work could be done. We all liked to get home for Christmas, too, although the boat ride from Lewisporte to Fogo Island in late December could be quite rough. I emptied my stomach many a time on that run.

Mrs. Wilhelmina (Payne) Mercer, who lived on Allandale Road in St. John's, did my laundry, mending and darning for the full five years I attended Queen's. Following a basketball game in the RCMP gym on Kenna's Hill on a Saturday afternoon, I would walk to the Mercer home on Allandale Road, deposit and pick up laundry, and sometimes stay for a hearty supper.

Canon Meaden, the principal, was more than kind to me, as he was to others. For summer employment he secured a position for me with Harvey's Travel Agency in St. John's. For two summers, 1953 and 1954, I worked there answering the telephone when in the office and making daily deposits of money to the bank on Water Street and paying bills at various locations in town. A staff person from the office would drive me to the bank with the deposit and leave me to do the remainder of the work on foot. During those summers I boarded with Mrs. Gertrude Garland on Bond Street. For the summer of 1955 I was fortunate enough to get a job with a mineral prospecting company. Our party of five spent the summer of 1955 in the interior of Newfoundland prospecting for mineral deposits. Besides being provided for, even to a down-filled sleeping bag, I was paid $200 a month. Two hundred dollars in 1955 was a lot of money!

The work of prospecting in the bush, in Central Newfoundland during the summer of 1955, involved being flown inland, setting up camp near a pond or lake, and working in that area for a couple of weeks before being uprooted and flown to another destination. The work of prospecting involved a lot of footwork. With the use of a compass, our boss, Robert Wall, charted the way. From our starting point on the lake we spent the whole day travelling and collecting rock samples from the various outcrops along the way. We changed course a couple of times during the day, which eventually brought us back to our starting point on the lake. This was called a "traverse." After being in college all year without a lot of physical exercise, the first traverse was a difficult one. I figured we would never get back to camp. It got easier as time went on and I got in better physical shape.

Bishop Abraham died, rather suddenly, December 24, 1955. At a special electoral synod in the spring of 1956, Canon J. A. Meaden, principal of Queen's College, was elected to succeed him as diocesan bishop. It was fairly common practice at Queen's College for the more senior theological students to be appointed as student ministers, in some of the large, spread-out rural parishes that needed help, for summer ministry. Approaching the summer of 1956, Canon Meaden, the bishop-elect, still the principal of Queen's College, sent me to Happy Valley–Goose Bay, Labrador, as a student minister.

The old Queen's College, Forest Road, St. John's

Queen's College chapel

Left: Rev. Canon J. A. Meaden, principal of Queen's College
Right: Mrs. Flora Furze, Fogo, my friend and supporter

Mrs. Beatrice Meaden, wife of Bishop John Meaden, with her Queen's boys.
Left to right: Stewart Payne, Gordon Pevie, Mrs. Meaden, and James Coffin.

CHAPTER EIGHT
STUDENT MINISTER IN HAPPY VALLEY

In the summer of 1956 I entered yet another new world. Flying up to Labrador from Torbay Airport via Maritime Central Airways, passengers as well as luggage were weighed in. It was on my birthday, June 6, that I flew into Goose Bay for the first time, where the ground was still covered with snow. It was a light snowfall that didn't last all that long. Whatever advance communications were made, they hadn't worked very well because there was no one at the airport to meet me and take me over to Happy Valley. However, Tom Pardy was at the airport, expecting the arrival of an insurance agency representative. Tom greeted me as if I might be that person. When it was certain that the insurance agent was not on the plane, Tom took me with him to Happy Valley and to his home.

Today, Happy Valley is the headquarters of the Parish of Lake Melville. Happy Valley in 1956 was part of the Mission of Sandwich Bay, 200 miles inland from Cartwright, the headquarters of the vast mission that included several communities along the southern Labrador Coast as well. At the best of times the priest in Cartwright could make only a limited number of visits a year to Happy Valley. Archdeacon Lewis Norman made periodic visits to Happy Valley and Deaconess Chloe Adam spent the winter of 1955–1956 in Happy Valley.

Happy Valley was very much a young, rapidly growing frontier town on the edge of the American and Canadian military bases in Goose Bay. Only fourteen or fifteen years earlier, during the construction phases of the military bases, men started to come to the area looking for employment with the construction companies. I had the pleasure of getting to know the first three pioneer settlers from northern Labrador: Gilbert Saunders, John Broomfield, and Thorwald Perrault. I heard their stories of how they put up their tents on the bank of the Hamilton River in 1943, about five miles from the American base. They brought their families and went on to build their houses, often by lamplight, while working on the base all day. It wasn't long before others in like circumstances joined them and the community was on its way. In 1946, the Royal Canadian Air Force (RCAF) engineered a road through to Happy Valley, which made for a simpler and easier mode of transportation, especially for people working on the bases. Happy Valley is all sand. It must have been part of the Hamilton River riverbed centuries ago. With a bulldozer, roadways are fairly easily opened up.

Happy Valley was in 1956 and still is, I expect, a very cosmopolitan town: people from several different countries and places lived side by side, many from different parts of Newfoundland and Labrador. Some work seasonally and return home, others work on to retirement, but most people make Happy Valley their permanent home.

There was no Anglican clergy parsonage. Housing in Happy Valley in those days was a real concern. Families who had houses very likely had another family or individuals staying with them as they began work in Goose Bay and started to build for themselves. For the first couple of weeks I stayed with Tom and Alice Pardy, lived out of my suitcase, slept in their living room, on their chesterfield, and took meals with them. When school was out I took over a small room adjacent to the chapel in the Anglican-Moravian school as an all-purpose room and bedroom while going to the Pardys' for meals. Attached to the school was a small apartment for the school principal and family. Harold Lawrence, the principal, and his wife, Louise, with their young son Michael, were staying on through the summer awaiting the birth of another child. I was glad that Harold and Louise were there and grateful for their companionship, support, and an occasional meal.

Left: Arch of welcome for Lieutenant-Governor McPherson (summer 1956)
Right: Stewart (1956) on the front steps of Tom and Alice Pardy's house, with their two young daughters Marilyn and Glenda

The Anglican-Moravian school in Happy Valley and a large group of children gathered to meet and welcome Lieutenant-Governor McPherson, 1956

I was given to understand that somewhere along the way there was an agreement between the Anglicans and Moravians that, where the Anglican population in a community predominated, the Moravian Church stayed away and encouraged the few Moravians to worship with the Anglicans. Likewise, where the Moravian population in a community was predominant, the Anglican Church stayed away and encouraged the few Anglicans to worship with the Moravians. It might just have been a local understanding. I don't know. The Moravians laid claim to the ministry of bishops as well. By 1956 there were significant numbers of Anglicans and Moravians in Happy Valley. The Moravians already had their own church building and were about to build a house in anticipation of having a resident clergyman. Instead of building separate schools in Happy Valley, the Anglican and Moravian congregations combined their resources and built the one school known as the Anglican-Moravian school.

The Anglican congregation made arrangements for a chapel in the school. One wing of the school had two classrooms separated by folding doors. The chapel consisted of a small area at the end of one classroom separated from the classroom by folding doors and housing an altar, lectern, and prayer desk. On Saturdays we rearranged the classroom, put the desks back to the walls, cleaned the floor, placed the chairs in rows, opened the doors to the little sanctuary, and had our chapel ready for Sunday worship.

Several of the school board members had formed a theatre company. In the process of building a theatre they continued to show movies, western movies for the most part, in the same part of the school where the chapel and my room were. It was difficult to access the room on movie nights. The windows and doors were without screens. On movie nights particularly, mosquitoes got into my room and kept me awake for a good part of the night.

Canon Meaden, bishop-elect, had instructed me that I should not get involved in administration and school board matters, but do Sunday services, matins and evensong, visit families, help in any other ways I could, and find out whether the time had come for them to have a resident priest.

The pattern of church attendance was not great that summer. The weekends were the only time people had off from work on the military bases, and they had to take advantage of that time, in the short construction season, to build their own homes and property and help one another in the process. Summertime is holiday time, too, and many people were away. Sunday seemed to be no different from any other day of the week. Saws and hammers could be heard all around.

Coming from theological school, where we had church services, not only on Sunday at the cathedral but several times each day of the week in the college chapel, it was frustrating and disappointing not to find more people in attendance. More than once I stood in that school chapel and said to myself, "What am I doing here? What is it all about?" It was indeed on-the-job training, and I began to learn that ministry has its joys and satisfactions but also its frustrations and disappointments. One cannot always see immediately the fruit of one's labours.

So, for the whole summer of 1956 in Happy Valley I went door to door, walking all the way, and compiled a first-time list of more than 200 Anglican families. The anticipation of meeting new people, sharing their joys and sorrows, and discovering some ways in which I could be of service to them was great.

I must pay tribute to one dear lady, Kirkina Mucko. Kirkina had grown up in a family somewhere in the Rigolet area, where they moved from a summer fishing location to a winter location. One year when Kirkina was about two years of age, the family was alone in the winter location. Her mother was about to have a baby, so her father went off to fetch the midwife. Soon after he left home, a storm blew in and he was delayed longer than expected. He arrived home to find that the baby had come and little Kirkina had two frozen feet and legs. The end result was that he amputated her legs below the knees, then stood her in flour to stop the bleeding. As a young woman she married and had a family. I don't recall when she acquired her artificial limbs, but I imagine she lived some years without them.

Kirkina's husband died when the Spanish flu struck the Labrador Coast around 1918, and with no clergyman around at the time, she had him buried, reading the burial rite herself. Thirty-eight years a widow, Kirkina was now living with her daughter and son-in-law, Tom and Elsa Connuck, in Happy Valley. She was always so appreciative of a visit from "her minister." She worked in the home and did housework two or three days a week for Tom and Alice Pardy, with whom I was staying. It was a gift to hear Kirkina's story and the stories of others: stories of isolation, deprivation, and hardship, as well as stories of adventure, success, and accomplishments. My experiences in the summer of 1956 assured me, beyond the shadow of a doubt, that my future would always be in pastoral ministry.

Kirkina Mucko. Taken on the boardwalk leading up to the Hudson's Bay Company store in Rigolet before she had her prosthesis.

CHAPTER NINE
FINAL YEAR AT QUEEN'S COLLEGE AND ORDINATION

At the end of the summer of 1956, I went back home to Fogo and took Mother from the hospital there, where she had been diagnosed as having very bad diabetes and other complications, to the General Hospital in St. John's, then moved into Queen's College myself. Since Happy Valley would be without a resident ordained person for the winter, I went to Bishop-Elect Meaden and offered to go back to Happy Valley, do my last year of study on my own, then come back to St. John's in the spring for exams and ordination as a deacon. He appreciated my concern but said that I needed to be in the college for my final year. When Mother was discharged from hospital, I took her home to Fogo and came back to Queen's for my fifth and final year.

In 1952, five years was a long time to look forward to, but now, on the home stretch and with excitement mounting daily, it didn't seem so very long. The five years at MUN and in residence at Queen's College were among the best years of my life. In the fifth year, classes, study, and chapel services continued as usual. Bishop-Elect Meaden was still the principal of Queen's but was naturally taken up more with diocesan affairs and unable to be present for lectures every day as in other years. He made up for that by giving us mimeographed notes of his lectures so that we could study on our own. The course load was all at Queen's in our final year 1957, with no classes at MUN.

As a result of being a student minister in Happy Valley during the summer of 1956, my board and lodging at Queen's was covered in full for my final year. The principal administered funds that had been bequeathed to Queen's for student aid, and Bishop-Elect Meaden saw fit to help me as he had helped others. I can never doubt the fact that generosity is one of the characteristics of our loving God, and His gifts of generosity come to us through other people and varied circumstances.

The big event during the fall semester was Canon J. A. Meaden's consecration as bishop of Newfoundland, October 28, 1956, on the Feast of St. Simon and St. Jude, apostles. This took place at the Cathedral Church of St. John the Baptist in St. John's. Being his students, we had prime seats and were very much a part of this interesting and exciting service, the ordination and consecration of a bishop.

St. Mary's Church in St. John's had taken on the young, rapidly growing community of Mount Pearl as part of their parish. The folks in Mount Pearl built their own church, the Church of the Advent. St. Mary's was without an assistant priest for a while, and so by mutual agreement the senior students at Queen's College would help out. David Pearce, Gordon Pevie, Jim Coffin, Fred Haines, and I would preach and assist at the Sunday morning worship services. This was a good opportunity for us to get some on-the-job training. Queen's wasn't doing much at that time by way of sermon preparation and delivery, so we welcomed the opportunity. We each prepared a sermon and, in turn, delivered it the Sunday on duty, and on Monday morning, in class at Queen's, we underwent an evaluation of the sermon and delivery. Students who had heard the sermon offered their comments and criticisms. This was very helpful. I preached my first sermon in the Church of the Advent in Mount Pearl, using from Psalm 119, Verse 105, the text, "Your word is a lamp to my feet and a light to my path." I continued with the Sunday school Bible class in the Cathedral of St. John the Baptist parish hall on Sunday afternoons.

The Reverend Mr. Templeton, hospital chaplain in St. John's, was involved in a car accident while walking down Forest Road on his way to the General Hospital. As a result, I was asked, along with other theological students, to do some hospital visiting at the old General

Hospital on Forest Road, not far from Queen's. An added incentive was the prospect of seeing some of our female friends who were nurses-in-training.

In the orthopaedic wing of the old General Hospital there were long, open wards, ten or twelve beds to a ward. I got to know Simeon Spencer, a patient from Pushthrough, really well. Simeon had contracted polio and was paralyzed from the neck down. He had limited use of his arms and hands only. The hospital staff had to do everything for him, dress and undress him, put him in bed and take him out. He spent his days in a wheelchair. If his foot slipped off the footrest, someone had to lift it back up for him. His mind was good. He could read from a book if someone opened it up and placed it in front of him. In the course of my time at the hospital, I would visit other patients first and come back to Simeon and give him the extra time I had left. Simeon had deep insight into our human nature. In the course of conversation one afternoon he said, "You know, Stewart, I have so much to be thankful for." I thought to myself, *If you, in this condition, have so much to be thankful for, how much do I have to be thankful for?* I have never forgotten his words. I reflect on them again and again.

Mother's health was such now that she couldn't manage on her own alone and was living part of the year with Cyril, and part of the year with Mabel in Fogo. The time had come to sell the family home. The real estate market in Fogo was not great. She practically gave it away by today's standards, but a portion of the proceeds afforded some support and help to me.

As the year progressed, excitement grew with respect to ordination and to what parishes we might be sent. In more reflective moments, self-examination occupied our minds. I gave time, thought, and prayer to the questions in the Book of Common Prayer (BCP) service, *The Ordering of Deacons*, especially to the first two questions: "Do you trust that you are inwardly moved by the Holy Ghost to take upon you this office and administration, to serve God, for the promotion of His glory, and the edifying of His people?" and "Do you think that you are truly called, according to the will of our Lord Jesus Christ, and the due order of this Church, to the ministry of the Church?"

Five of us who were ordained as deacons in 1957. Left to right: Fred Haines, David Pearce, Stewart Payne, James Coffin, and Gordon Pevie.

Mrs. Wilhelmina (Payne) Mercer, right, with her sister and brother

These are awesome questions, which we would respond to not only once, on the day of ordination, but every day for the rest of our lives. There were other examiners along the way: the staff at Queen's College, and the bishop, who had the final say—to ordain or not to ordain. In the final analysis, the five of us were prepared to answer the above questions with, "I trust so," and "I think so."

Upon reflection, I can say that the staff of Queen's College had seriously taken their task to offer the best preparation for ordained ministry, concentrating on spiritual development and the core functions of ministry: liturgical worship, preaching, organizing, and exercising pastoral care. Yet no theological college can ever fully prepare one for all the eventualities in a lifetime of ministry, in the world beyond the college. The college work is well done if it has given to its students the tools to keep on learning, and to do critical study and reflection, which is a lifelong pursuit.

The critical time for the five of us—David, Jim, Gordon, Fred, and me—as for all deacons and priests, would be when we were out in the parish, dealing with people in life-and-death situations, sharing their joys and sorrows. How do I explain the Scriptures so that they speak relevantly to people today, how can I help this troubled teenager, this person or family grieving the death of a loved one? Caught up in the emotions of a tragic situation, how do I, at the same time, celebrate with young parents the birth of their first-born child? What matters most out there is who a priest is as a person, and how a priest identifies with people and provides help from his or her own inner resources, witnessing to God's great love for all.

As the day of my ordination neared, I acquired the appropriate clerical dress. Because of my height, and pride, I suspect, I was not keen on the thought of wearing a black top hat, but believing that it might be a requirement, I gave in and went downtown alone one day and bought the hat. My sister-in-law Edna made my four stoles and gave them to me as an ordination gift.

I completed the studies for the Bachelor of Arts and the Licentiate in Theology degrees. Because our ordination exams were set and corrected in England, the final results would not arrive in time for the

1957 spring convocations at MUN and Queen's College. Graduation exercises would follow in the spring of 1958.

The big day finally came, Sunday, June 23, 1957, when five of us—David Pearce, Gordon Pevie, Jim Coffin, Fred Haines, and I—were made deacons in the Cathedral Church of St. John the Baptist, St. John's, by Bishop J. A. Meaden. This special life-changing event was made all the more memorable because Mother was able to attend the ordination. She had been a patient in the General Hospital in St. John's again that spring and was discharged in time to attend the ordination. I have always suspected that she might have asked to be discharged from hospital in order to be sure of getting to the service. It was so special to have her there. The times when Mother was in St. John's waiting to be admitted to hospital, and upon being discharged from hospital, she stayed at the home of Gladys (Pomeroy) Windsor, who was originally from Fogo. Gladys was such a loving and caring individual.

Left: Stewart and mother, following ordination as a deacon, in front of Cyril's house in Fogo. Right: Stewart, circa 1958.

A day or so after the ordination, there was the appointment with Bishop Meaden regarding parish placement. During my appointment, Bishop Meaden asked me what I thought of going back to Happy Valley. My response was that I felt it was a place for an experienced priest. To this he replied, "I would like to appoint you to Happy Valley."

I could only reply, "The bishop's wish is my command." And so it was that I looked forward to returning to the people and place that I had grown to love and respect so much.

Before taking up our appointments, we were given a few days holiday. I took Mother back to Fogo and spent a few days with family and friends. One day I went over to Wild Cove, Seldom-Come-By, where I had spent my first year as a teacher, to visit Uncle Bill and Aunt Emma Combden, with whom I had boarded in 1949–1950. Uncle Bill asked me where I had been and what I had done in the meantime. I told him how I had gone to another summer school, spent five years as a student at MUN and Queen's College, and was just recently made a deacon. He listened intently, and when I finished he took his pipe out of his mouth and exclaimed, "Well, you must know it all now." I might have agreed somewhat had not our retreat conductor reminded us that, following those years of study, our education was about to begin. In short, I would be on my way to Happy Valley.

CHAPTER TEN
MINISTRY IN HAPPY VALLEY–GOOSE BAY, 1957–1965

Following the short holiday, the newly ordained deacons were off to their appointments: David Pearce to Port aux Basques, James Coffin to Bay L'Argent, Fred Haines to Change Islands, Gordon Pevie and me to the Mission of Sandwich Bay. Gordon and I boarded the SS *Kyle* in St. John's for the week-long trip to Labrador.

In those days some of the fishermen from Newfoundland, especially from Conception Bay, would go down to the Labrador Coast for the summer cod fishery. At several ports of call we took aboard a number of fishermen, their families, their fishing gear, and whatever else they would need for the summer. At practically every port of call, day or night, the steamer's whistle alerted the people and the dogs. The dogs would howl for the longest time.

People came out to the *Kyle* in their motorboats and punts to collect mail and freight, as well as to pick up and drop off passengers. It was interesting to watch. In the course of the day, whenever the *Kyle* was approaching a settlement, Gordon and I were on deck to see the places and people and what was going on. The weather was good and we enjoyed the trip so much. One tourist we met on board, the Reverend Mr. Wood, an Episcopal priest from the United States, later sent Bishop Meaden $20 to be divided between Gordon and me.

Gordon disembarked in Cartwright and I continued on to Goose Bay. At the dock in Goose Bay I met Hayward Bird, who was there with a truck collecting an item of freight. He kindly gave me a lift to Happy Valley.

Previous to my arrival in Happy Valley, the Reverend F. W. Peacock, superintendent of the Moravian Mission in Labrador, and his wife, Doris, had moved from Nain to Happy Valley, Bill to be the Moravian minister in Happy Valley, and Doris to be principal of the Anglican-Moravian school in Happy Valley. They were occupying the small apartment at the Anglican-Moravian school. School not being in session during the summer, I moved into the same small room at the school that I had occupied the previous summer and took my meals with Tom and Alice Pardy.

The very first morning I was awakened early by a knock on the door. On answering the call I was surprised to find the Reverend William Peacock kindly bringing me a cup of tea. It was a real teacup and not a mug. I was mystified, because I was not familiar with the apparent English custom of having a cup of tea in bed before rising and getting dressed. I accepted his kindness with gratitude for a few mornings, then graciously declined because I didn't expect him to be tending on me like that. I was very much his junior and it didn't seem right that he should be doing that for me.

When school opened in September I couldn't very well be going in and out of the classroom during the day to get to my room, and besides, in school season, the room was there for the teacher's use. After every attempt to find a boarding house failed, I approached Sampson Learning, one of the churchwardens, with my dilemma, which was so dire that I would not be able to stay the winter if more appropriate accommodations could not be found. After breaking down all his arguments about the service he could offer not being good enough for the minister, he offered me his family's one and only spare room, their small sitting room. I will always be grateful to Sampson and Ethel and their family for taking me in and giving me the best they had.

For the next four years that small room at Sampson and Ethel's place was my bedroom, washroom, study, and office. Indoor plumbing and running water had not yet arrived. The toilet facility was an outhouse, down in the garden, which was hard to reach in the winter through the deep snow. Sometimes it was impossible to close the outhouse door because of the snow and the buildup of ice, so an alternative had to be found. I soon discovered who had indoor bathroom facilities and where I was welcome to visit. My room was heated with a small oil space heater that had a fuel tank on the back of it which had to be refilled rather frequently in the winter. The oil drained from a forty-five-gallon drum out in the yard.

St. Andrew's new church, Happy Valley, ready for dedication by Bishop Meaden, 1959. Note the welcome arch on the church front.

The room didn't lend itself as an office. If someone wanted to see me I would have to go to them instead of inviting them to my room. From time to time an official from the base or a visitor to Goose Bay would make a courtesy call on the clergy in Happy Valley. If I knew that in advance, I would arrange to meet them with the United Church minister at the United Church manse.

I hadn't been back as a deacon in Happy Valley long before becoming acquainted with Jim and Rhoda Bailey. Jim was a customs officer in Goose Bay. They lived in the Department of Transport (DOT) area and, like a number of other families in the DOT, became quite interested and involved in the work of the church in Happy Valley. All the while I was without a vehicle, Jim Bailey, along with John Pardy, the welfare officer, were always available to give me a lift. Rhoda did my laundry every week from 1957 to 1962 before I moved into the new rectory. Whenever I deposited or picked up laundry I was able to take a shower and have a meal. If it wasn't mealtime when I arrived, Rhoda would always say, "What would you like, a cup of tea or a glass of milk?"

The Anglican rectory in Happy Valley, built in the summer of 1961. I took occupancy in January 1962.

My stock answer, in fun, was "both," and I would receive both.

Some years after my time in Happy Valley, Jim and Rhoda retired to their new home in Embree, Newfoundland. I kept in touch, seeing them when visiting my sister Beatie in Lewisporte. Some years after Jim's death, Rhoda moved into a seniors' home in Grand Falls. Again, when I was passing through Grand Falls we would stop to visit Rhoda. On one occasion, we reflected long on our years in Goose Bay and then took our leave. But there was something I felt that I should have shared with Rhoda while I had the opportunity. I hadn't gone far from Grand Falls, so I turned around and went back to the home again. Rhoda was surprised and wondered what had caused my return. I then said to her, "Rhoda, there is something I should have told you before, and it is this. You and Jim made all the difference to my stay and ministry in Happy Valley. I could never have done it without all that you and Jim did for me throughout those years." It was an emotional moment, but one that needed to be faced and owned.

Left: Selma, Stewart, and Uncle John Martin, who turned the sod for the new church. Photo taken in the rectory at Happy Valley. Right: Aunt Mae Pardy, my housekeeper, winter of 1962, Happy Valley.

Stewart's first car. Happy Valley, in front of Sampson Learning's house, where I boarded for four years.

There hadn't been a resident Anglican clergy in Happy Valley prior to my arrival. Curious to know what the new minister looked like, Bella Brown asked another lady, "Have you seen the new minister?"

"Yes."

"What does he look like?"

"Well, if you see a black suit of clothes going down the road with nothing in it, that's him."

I mentioned earlier my concern about wearing a black top hat because of my height, but I felt that it was expected of me. Walking down Hamilton River Road one day, soon after I arrived I stopped to chat with some young boys who were playing by the roadside. It was difficult to get much conversation going; they kept laughing and looking up at me. To my question, "What are you laughing at?" one little fellow looked at me and asked quite innocently, "Are you a cowboy, sir?" I never wore the hat after that.

The Mission of Sandwich Bay became two missions in 1957: the Mission of Cartwright and the Mission of Happy Valley. The Mission of Happy Valley consisted of Happy Valley, the headquarters, Mud Lake, North West River, and Rigolet. In the Rigolet area there were several little places where people fished on the coast in summer and moved inland in the winter to hunt and trap.

The whole of the Strait of Belle Isle and Labrador were one deanery, a subdivision of a diocese. It is easy to imagine the cost and difficulty of bringing clergy of this large area together for a deanery meeting. I can recall only two such meetings during my time in Labrador. We met once as a deanery when all the clergy were together at Killdevil Camp in Lomond, Bonne Bay, for some other meetings, and once in St. Anthony.

The Reverend Martin Mate, priest in charge of the Mission of St. Anthony, and rural dean of the deanery of the Strait of Belle Isle and Labrador, later bishop of Eastern Newfoundland and Labrador, once called us all together in St. Anthony. I left Goose Bay on the coastal steamer. Gordon Pevie joined me in Cartwright and we proceeded to St. Anthony. It was great to get out of our isolation and be together with one another. What was most important was not the business of the meeting but the fellowship, of being able to say our prayers together and hear one another.

Members of the "Anglican Young People's Association," circa 1957–1958

The Anglican Young People's Association staging a play

The Reverend Carl Major, priest in charge of the Mission of Battle Harbour, attended the deanery meeting in St. Anthony. For some time Carl had been convinced that the Battle Harbour Mission could best be served with the use of a small aircraft. Carl trained and obtained his pilot's licence, and the Diocese of Newfoundland purchased a Super Piper Cub aircraft and made it available to him, and Carl became known as the flying priest. Following the deanery meeting in St. Anthony, Carl, having business to attend to in Goose Bay, gave me a lift back home. On the way to Goose Bay, Carl landed the plane in Mary's Harbour, where he and his wife, Norma, and family lived. I had the opportunity to visit a few friends and spend some time with Carl and Norma before going on to Goose Bay.

In the days of denominational education in Newfoundland, clergy were quite involved as members of school boards and in the administration of schools. It was not uncommon for the local clergy to give a hand with the teaching of religious education courses as well. This was very much the case in Happy Valley. When I arrived in 1957, board members informed me that the jobs of chairman and secretary treasurer of the Anglican-Moravian school board were mine. I had nightmares at first because of my inexperience, and I begged the previous chairman to carry on a little longer, so that I could learn the ropes. The decision was final: it was my work and responsibility. I took it on and gave it all I could.

The school board had done a good job without the support of a resident clergyperson, and the result was a five-classroom Anglican-Moravian school. In the meantime, the school population was growing rapidly because of people coming to work in Goose Bay. This meant that we had to find an extra classroom or two every summer to accommodate new students. Besides the role of seeing to classroom construction, I was to find and employ teachers, find boarding houses for them, administer the finances, including the teachers' payroll, and on occasion do manual work around the property. At times I felt that I was giving more time and energy to school work than to church work. Looking back, I see it all as ministry to people, especially to children.

In such a church-run school system, nearly all the teachers

applied their gifts and talents wherever the need, in church as well as in school, as an organist, lay reader, and as a Sunday school teacher. We just took it for granted that the teachers would do those things.

In June of 1958, all five deacons—Gordon, David, Fred, Jim, and I—were back to St. John's preparing for our ordination. On June 8, 1958, Bishop J. A. Meaden ordained us priests in the Cathedral Church of St. John the`Baptist. At the same time I was able to attend diocesan synod, as well as MUN and Queen's convocations, for the conferring of the B.A. and L.Th. degrees.

The Anglican-Moravian school was one of the few public buildings in Happy Valley. It was used not only as a school and a chapel for Anglicans but for all sorts of social events and fundraisers, dances, card games, and various evening meetings. One parishioner had a problem with what he called his church being used for all those social activities. He came to see me soon after I arrived and asked that I would stop all those activities in the church. We talked for hours over a period of days, and when he realized that I couldn't do that, even if I wanted to, he became very antagonistic, and thereafter did much to annoy me.

On one of his afternoon visits to me, he threatened to stop the dance scheduled for that night. I discouraged him all I could and assured him that I would not be responsible for what might happen if he tried to stop it. However, when I went up to open the school for the Anglican Church Women (ACW), who were sponsoring the dance, there he was at the door. We shared a few words, and after a while he went away. About midnight, when the dance was in full swing, he came back, marched up through the crowd, and pushed his box of offering envelopes at me, vowing that he was through and would have nothing else to do with us. A few days later he requested a refund of his offerings to the church that year. We didn't have to refund free-will offerings, but we did. The select vestry agreed, for peace and quiet, and the treasurer sent him a cheque for $25. In the meantime, whenever I visited families in his area, I tried to visit him, although he would disappear the minute I entered his abode. Wherever and whenever I met him, I greeted him, although he would turn away and ignore me. When I sent out a letter to the parishioners I made sure that he received his copy as well.

This standoff relationship went on for a couple of years. Finally, on November 30, 1960, it changed. We were celebrating St. Andrew's Day and the first anniversary of our new church. After the early morning celebration of Holy Communion, I went across to the post office before going to breakfast. As I was coming out of the post office, Ron was going in. As I greeted him, he passed me an envelope, which I gratefully accepted. Back in my room, on opening the envelope, I found his thank-offering envelope with $50 in it and the old, refunded cheque for $25. I was elated. This meant a change of heart and attitude. I telephoned him immediately. Anticipating my call, he answered on the first ring. I told him how I felt, that he had really made my day.

"Yes," he said, "I have had a change of heart and attitude. I couldn't go anywhere else—meaning to another church—and I couldn't stay away any longer because you never let me go."

After that, wherever he saw me he greeted me like a long-lost brother. It was an added joy to see him in one of the back seats in the new St. Andrew's Church from time to time.

A few years later I was called to an emergency situation at the nursing station, only to find that Ron had suffered a severe heart attack. He was in an oxygen tent. I held his hand and said a prayer. Soon after that, he slipped away.

For the first couple of years I had to rely on other people when I needed car transportation. Minnie Davis, born and raised in Labrador, was nursing in the hospital on the American base. Her family was living next door to my boarding house. Quite often, when she came to visit her parents, she made her car available to me if I needed it. Minnie married Steven Harper, whom she met in Goose Bay. They made their home in Richardson, Texas, where Steven had some family members and relatives. We have kept in touch to this day.

The military bases in Goose Bay had their chaplains but, in the absence of an Anglican chaplain, on the first Sunday in the month I presided at a Holy Communion service in the chapel on the American base and the last Sunday in the month I presided at a Holy Communion service in the chapel on the Canadian base. I was always appreciative for this exposure to new experiences and situations with people from other places. Friendships were formed that lasted long after moving away from Goose Bay. For some time I was part of a team that played basketball in the gymnasium on the Canadian base.

Eventually the Hudson's Bay Company (HBC) brought in a few small German cars, the NSU Prinz. I bought one for the sum of $500. It had a high-powered motor in the rear. People couldn't understand how I could fit into it. Muriel Way used to call it a vacuum cleaner. There were no paved roads in Happy Valley then. After a heavy rain or melting snow and ice, the roads were full of ruts and water holes. It was hard on the little car. It would often cut out, causing me to push it aside and wait for the motor to dry off. I graduated to a Volkswagen bug, which after a couple of years I traded in for another Volkswagen bug. The price of the second Volkswagen was $1,895, toward which I received a trade-in of $1,233 for my old one. I still have the invoice to show. I also have a slip that shows that the minimum, annual clergy salary in 1960 was $2,700. It wasn't that cars were cheap in those days; salaries were very different, evening things out.

Happy Valley was certainly finding its growing pains in those days. Young individuals and young families came to Goose Bay to find employment. The fast pace of life led to problems for some who were not prepared for that environment. Bishop Meaden once reminded me that some of the problems were due partly to the fact that there were very few grandparents in the new and rapidly growing community. I assume that what he meant by that was that if grandparents were around they would solve a lot of problems by being able to care for the children when both young parents were working outside the home. I can imagine, too, that Bishop Meaden felt that grandparents would have a steadying and grounding influence on the younger generation in this frontier town.

All through my university days and in Happy Valley I kept in touch with Mother and the family in Fogo through letter writing. As time went on, Mother's letters were showing signs that her sight was deteriorating. She ultimately became blind. When letter writing was no longer possible for her, I assured her that, whether she could reply to my letters or not, I would still write to her, even more often. I already had a small tape recorder and some tapes, so I began to record my voice and our news and send her the tapes. She had access to a tape machine and with help from a family member would listen to the tapes over and over again and do a recording of her voice and news in return. I still have one tape with a recording from her.

During several of the eight years I spent in Happy Valley we had a youth group called the Anglican Young People's Association. They were mature young adults from the community—some teachers, some HBC staff, and a nurse from the nursing station. One of the things we took on to do year after year was to stage a play. That entailed a lot of work, practising for a period of time, building a makeshift stage in the school, and putting off the play several times. Lots of fun and good fellowship kept us together and involved in the life of the church.

A priest's role is multifaceted. While not a businessman, one had to attend to a lot of business. When I went to Happy Valley in 1957, the Diocese of Newfoundland was gearing up for an advance appeal toward financial and spiritual renewal, called the Newfoundland Forward Canvass. The Wells Organization was the professional fundraiser company. The appeal was commonly referred to as the Wells Campaign. Here is a short quote from one of the letters Bishop Meaden sent out to all the parishes. "I call upon every parish and mission, every congregation and individual throughout the whole diocese, to regard this greatest effort in our history as a challenge to show by your gifts what your faith and your Church mean to you."

I didn't feel that the fledgling little Mission of Happy Valley, just coming into existence, without an identity, without a church building of our own, without a clergy residence, or anything else, should be involved in this appeal. We really had to start from scratch, in a sense, to plant the church first. Bishop Meaden understood our situation and allowed me to pursue first things first.

The big challenge in Happy Valley was to grow the church as far as people were concerned, to have our own place of worship and a house for the priest to live in. Knowing about the living conditions, Bishop

Meaden wanted me to get on quickly with the erection of a rectory. The need for a residence was great, but I was single and could manage where I was a little longer. The need for a church building was greater because it would address the needs of many more people. By this time the congregation had grown to the point that the chapel in the Anglican-Moravian school was inadequate, even as we opened into a second classroom.

We set ourselves the task of building the church building first. By the generous, free labour of Harold Merry, an architect on the Canadian military base in Goose Bay, a blueprint was drawn up and eventually approved by the diocesan executive committee in St. John's. How excited I was the day when I joined in with members of our local organization, "The Brotherhood of Anglican Churchmen (BAC)," to clear the site for the new church, on land we already owned, adjacent to the Anglican-Moravian school. I was more excited still when, one spring day, the congregation gathered for the sod-turning ceremony. Amidst hymns and prayers, Uncle John Martin, the oldest member of the congregation, turned the sod, assisted by a number of the youngest members of the congregation scooping up the sand with their spoons. This was followed by a reception and refreshments in the school.

With the help of a loan and a grant from the Anglican Foundation, a national church body, and a larger bank loan, the church building was erected in 1959 by E. S. Martin Construction Limited, from Rexdale, Ontario. Wally Brittain was the construction supervisor. The contract price for erecting the building was $55,000. This was the first building project I had had anything to do with. How I watched the progress, day by day, and frequently visited the site to see the unbelievable progress that was being made!

The cost of the building didn't include the furniture, such as an altar, pulpit, pews, prayer desks, and a font. The bishop had earlier promised me $6,000 of diocesan funds with which to build a house, the rectory. A telephone call to the bishop reluctantly freed up the $6,000 for church furnishings, on the condition that we would, over the winter, try to replace the $6,000 and proceed with the rectory in the spring. I gave him my word. The church furnishings, at a cost of $6,600 from Globe Furniture Company in Waterloo, Ontario, completed the church building, ready for dedication and use for worship. Bishop Meaden came in November 1959 for the dedication and official opening. It was very near the Feast of St. Andrew, the patron saint of my own home church in Fogo. At the bishop's suggestion the church building was dedicated with the name of St. Andrew. It was a very happy day when we were able to assemble in our own new church and offer our worship to God.

In Happy Valley, early on, I enrolled to study for the General Synod Bachelor of Divinity degree. It was difficult to obtain the prescribed texts and to find the time to study. It meant a lot of cramming during the weeks leading up to the exams. The Reverend Alec Smith, the United Church minister in Happy Valley, supervised my final exams. I did complete the program and was awarded the Bachelor of Divinity degree.

Jo Lutley, a nurse from England who had worked in the nursing station in Happy Valley for a few years, had moved on to a nursing station in Frobisher Bay, Northwest Territories (now Iqaluit, Nunavut). She wrote me to say that in Frobisher there was a young Anglican priest, Brian Gilbertson, his wife, and two young daughters. He was learning the Inuit language and getting on with his ministry, but Jo thought that a visit from another Anglican priest might be helpful to him. I wrote her to say that I would love to visit Frobisher and spend some time with the Gilbertsons if they so desired, but I couldn't, at this time, afford the cost of travel. I figured that was the end of that proposal. In return mail I received another letter from Jo with a cheque to cover the cost of a round trip from Goose Bay to Frobisher. In the letter she commented that since she hadn't given much to the church recently, she would now support some inter-diocesan travel. In the middle of the winter I spent a delightful week with Brian and his family in Frobisher, of as much benefit or more to me than to Brian.

Frobisher Bay (now Iqaluit) is beyond the treeline. Christmas trees, apart from artificial ones, were scarce. So, for several years after my visit with the Gilbertsons, a couple of weeks before Christmas I acquired two or three natural fir trees, wrapped them in burlap, and shipped them off to the parish in Frobisher Bay.

During the summer of 1961 we built the rectory in Happy Valley. When in town I was on that site every day to see the progress that the two carpenters, a Mr. Dalton and a Mr. Johnson from Catalina, Newfoundland, were making, and sometimes to drive a few nails myself.

After spending four years in one small room without some of the modern conveniences, I couldn't wait for that house to be completed. When it was nearing completion I moved in some of my few belongings. Then, one night in January 1962, when the painters had put on the finishing touches, I drove them home around midnight and came back for my first night in the new rectory. What an amazing change it was to be in a dwelling with a kitchen, dining room, sitting room, bedrooms, bathroom, and a study or office. I wasn't in any hurry to go to bed that unforgettable night. I kept going from one room to another, wondering if what I was seeing was real. It was almost too good to be true.

Aunt Mae Pardy, originally from Cartwright, Labrador, but then living with her daughter, Muriel Way and family, in Happy Valley, became my live-in housekeeper for the winter of 1962. Aunt Mae was a marvellous person, so kind, concerned, and caring for my welfare. The telephone would often ring at mealtimes because people knew I would be at home then. Aunt Mae would insist on taking the calls and, unless it was an emergency, inform the caller that I was at lunch or dinner and please leave a number or call back later. Having such an excellent housekeeper, that winter I was able to board the new principal of the Anglican-Moravian school, Mr. Fred Field, and his son Fred. The rectory also offered a welcome as a gathering place for some people, especially for some of the teachers living away from home and their families.

Because there was now a rectory, Selma Penney Carlson and I got married October 11, 1962. Two of our children, Carla and Christopher, were born while we were in Happy Valley.

Mrs. Bridget Somerton from Portugal Cove, Newfoundland, who came to work and live on the American base, was a frequent weekend visitor to the rectory. Bridget was a staunch churchgoer, had a powerful voice, and immediately became a choir member in St. Andrew's Church. She knew she was welcome and didn't need to wait for a special invitation. She came with her culinary and housekeeping skills, some supplies, and offered her help wherever needed.

I should also mention David Lawton, who worked with CBC and lived on base but came to church in Happy Valley. David's father, the Reverend Sidney Lawton, from England, was one time priest in charge of the Mission of Sandwich Bay. David became a very good friend and was one of the special attendants in our wedding party.

In November 1964, Bishop Meaden wrote me about a number of issues and concluded with this request: "You are aware, I am sure, that the deanery of the Strait of Belle Isle and Labrador has at present no rural dean [Martin Mate was no longer in St. Anthony] and the bishop would very much like to have one. Would it be asking too much of the Incumbent of Happy Valley to accept this responsibility, for a time at least?" I accepted to act as rural dean of the deanery of the Strait of Belle Isle and Labrador.

In July of 1964, Selma and I, with Carla, visited Mother and other relatives in Fogo. We were just back in Happy Valley for a week when I received the sad news that Mother had died. She had slipped away in her sleep unexpectedly. True to her wish, she never gave anyone much trouble. I was off to Fogo for her funeral, a celebration of her loving, caring, and devoted life.

I was chairman of the school board that was formed to get on with the work of building an amalgamated high school in Happy Valley. The building wasn't completed until sometime in the fall of 1965, after we had moved on to Bay Roberts, but I gladly accepted the invitation and went back for the official opening and dedication. That school, later on, was named the "F. W. Peacock Academy" after the Moravian minister in Happy Valley, the Reverend William Peacock, who took on as chairman of the board after me and saw the building project to completion.

CHAPTER ELEVEN
MINISTRY IN RIGOLET, NORTH WEST RIVER, MUD LAKE

Happy Valley was the headquarters of the mission and only part of my responsibilities and blessings. Rigolet is about 100 miles out Lake Melville east of Goose Bay. The Hudson's Bay Company (HBC) store was the hub of Rigolet and area in those days. In Rigolet, of the fifteen to twenty families, several were Inuit and others were settlers with mixed heritage. I always wished I could have learned to speak the Inuit language, but they all had a very good command of the English language, so there was no problem. The one-room school served as a chapel as well. Visitors to Rigolet, including the clergy, all stayed at the HBC manager's house, referred to by the folk in the community as the "Big House." I did on occasion change that tradition by staying with a local family, Lawrence and Nellie Flowers.

Rigolet was the terminus for the pilots who piloted large cargo ships to and from Goose Bay. There was also a forty-five-ton pilot boat that transported the pilots out to Rigolet to meet a ship and took them back to Goose Bay when they left a ship at Rigolet. There was also a small house in Rigolet where the pilots stayed, waiting the arrival of a ship or waiting for the pilot boat to take them back to Goose Bay.

My churchwarden in Happy Valley, Russell Chaulk, was one of the pilots. The other pilot was Baxter Pelley. Russell inquired if I might get a passage to Rigolet on one of the large cargo ships. The reply was that I would have to sign on as an apprentice pilot. I was not prepared to do that, but they took me anyway and treated me royally. I assume that they were not supposed to take passengers on those cargo ships. The crew would likely have thought that I was indeed an apprentice pilot. The irony was that I could be classified as a pilot of sorts, a pilot of people, maybe.

While on a visit to Rigolet in the summer I would see all the people as they came into the HBC store for supplies and stayed around for an evening church service. Each summer, I made the rounds on the HBC salmon collector boat to all the summer fishing places in the area. While the collectors were taking on the salmon, I would make a pastoral visit to the two or three families in the little cove or inlet, and off we would go to the next fishing place and do the same thing. During a visit to one little fishing station on one occasion, I was asked by a lady how I liked it there. Of course, I replied that I liked it all right and inquired how she liked it in such a remote and isolated spot. Her reply was that it was the best place in the world and that when she went into Rigolet for supplies she was mesmerized!

In winter the means of travel to Rigolet was by air, followed by a dog team trip to the several outlying winter places within a radius of fifty miles. My air travel was with whoever was going my way and willing to take me, sometimes on the Grenfell Mission plane. The welfare officer who chartered a plane to Rigolet in March each year was always willing to take me along. We would each hire a dog team and driver and make the rounds to the few families in the outlying region over a week or ten days, depending on the weather. My driver on several occasions was Ernest Pottle.

The one long-time teacher in the one-room school in Rigolet was Evelyn (Shiwak) Campbell, whom I first met when we were in summer school at MUN in St. John's in 1949.

Children from those outlying little places in the Rigolet area and on the northern Labrador Coast would normally go to North West River to the Grenfell Mission boarding school for their education. North West River had a fairly large amalgamated school named "Yale" and two residences for children, operated by the Grenfell Mission. Each residence had a house mother and appropriate domestic staff. The Grenfell

Mission, late in August, would collect the children who wanted to come to school, by boat or plane, and settle them in the residences for the school year. The children were not so cut off from their families because the Grenfell Mission had radio contact with all the nursing stations in the communities from where the children came, and the hospital in North West River was the regional hospital for folk in all those communities. Besides, parents were free to visit whenever they felt like it.

There were two little sisters, Sarah and Belinda Oliver, who lived with their father, John Oliver, brother Curtis, and their aged grandmother, Ann Oliver. The grandmother, since their mother had died, was very protective of the girls. Although they were of school age, she would not permit them to be taken away to North West River. I provided them with the appropriate school books from time to time, and Irene MacKenzie, who had had some schooling in North West River, helped them with their early education.

More than fifty years later, I made the inquiry and discovered that Sarah and Belinda were living in Rigolet. Sarah had married Garland Baikie and raised a family. Belinda had married Harry Shiwak and raised a family. I had a long, long telephone conversation with Sarah, which brought us both to tears at the end. Sarah and Belinda received no more formal schooling except through the help that Irene (MacKenzie) Oliver and I were able to provide, and night school in Rigolet they were able to attend for a couple of winters. Sarah is now a deacon in the Anglican Church and has a great ministry in the Rigolet area. Belinda is a significant leader, too, in the community and beyond.

The HBC in Rigolet had radio contact with the Grenfell Mission in North West River and would be informed that the welfare officer and the minister were on their way out the bay. People in those little winter places were never surprised when we turned up. They would be expecting us and would have a cooked meal ready. They were so glad to have a visitor. They were so delightful, welcoming, and hospitable. We each carried a food supply on the komatik—a long, low sled adopted in northern Newfoundland and especially in Labrador for winter travel and hauled by a team of dogs—and shared it with the people as they shared what they had with us.

Left to right: Ernest Pottle, my dog team driver, Stewart Payne, and Max Shiwak, having a mug-up on one of our dog team trips in the Rigolet area. Max was also the welfare officer's dog team driver.

Dog team travel in the Rigolet area

The welfare officer would do his business with them. I would conduct evening prayer after supper and Holy Communion in the morning before taking our leave for the next place. It was such a privilege and pleasure to be with those people, the salt of the earth kind of people, and to feel that genuine ministry was taking place. Sometimes they had to put up with us for several days because of bad weather. Only once did we have to stop along the way because of a snowstorm and spend the night in a tilt, which is a very small one-room shelter used while hunting and trapping animals.

One spring, at breakup time, I was stuck in Rigolet for nearly two weeks. At the end of that time I engaged a dog team to take me up the bay, following the shoreline on the ballicatters—ice formed by the action of spray and waves along the shoreline, making a fringe or band of ice on the landward side. We hadn't gone far when we saw a dog team coming toward us. We soon discovered that Bessie Mucko, from farther up the bay in a little place called Carrawalla, had died and the family was bringing her body to Rigolet for burial. So, of course, back we went to Rigolet with them for the funeral. By the time the funeral was over, the weather had cleared and the Grenfell Mission plane was out to do some business, so I got a ride back with them. I'll never know how the aborted dog team trip up the bay would have gone at that time of the year. It would not have been pleasurable.

Sometime in the late autumn of 1964, with a visit to the Rigolet area completed, I was awaiting transportation with anyone going in to Goose Bay. Some American personnel in a sizable metal boat came into Rigolet on their way to Goose Bay. I made my wants known, and they were willing to take me on board, provided that I didn't mind roughing it with them. We left Rigolet late in the afternoon. Part of the way up Lake Melville, the wind breezed up and the water became so rough that we had to put in under the lee of St. John's Island and wait out the breeze. After a couple of hours the wind seemed to have abated and the men decided to journey on. As we got out from the shelter of St. John's Island and on course, the wind was stronger than before. While we were pounding the rough waves, an electrical fire broke out on board. It was a frightening experience. The damage to the structure of the metal boat was not extensive, except we lost our lights and all navigational equipment. In the pitch-black darkness of night, without navigational equipment, the Americans, unfamiliar with the area, didn't know where we were. All they could do was keep the boat heading into the wind, and hope and pray that we could slowly ride the waves until daylight. It was a long and worrisome night as we kept peering into the darkness looking for signs of light on land. Many imaginary lights were seen. With morning light, the crew was able to pick up our bearings and go on to Goose Bay. All is well that ends well.

Some of the women in the Rigolet area made different items from a certain kind of sturdy grass found in the area: trays, bowls, and placemats. There wasn't much sale for those things in the Rigolet area, so I took it upon myself to be their agent in Goose Bay, where there was a much larger population and a better market. As I sold a few items, it meant a little more money for them. I still have two bowls and a tray that Aunt Ann Oliver gave me.

Some years the folks on the American base in Goose Bay did a Christmas toy drop from the air to the children in Rigolet. I have a feeling that the "drop" included more by way of Christmas gifts than just toys for the children.

I went to North West River once a month, usually travelling with the Grenfell Mission. There was no bridge over Goose River then and no bridge over North West River. In fact, the cable car across North West River, now replaced by a bridge, came after my time. The Grenfell Mission kept a truck across the river on the Innu side of North West River, which is now known as Sheshatshiu, and we crossed Goose River and North West River by boat and used the truck over the dirt road, which could be a bit rough at times. On my visits to North West River I stayed at the home of Dr. and Mrs. Anthony Paddon or in the hospital staff quarters.

As we approached North West River we first came to the Innu settlement of Sheshatshiu, on the bank of North West River. The Innu population was Roman Catholic. They had a resident priest, the Reverend Father Pearson, a church, a house for the priest, and a small school. The people lived in canvas tents, teepee style. It was during the late 1950s or early 1960s that they began to get standard housing. They traded across the river in North West River at the HBC store. It was still the custom for them to stock up in the fall at the HBC store and go back into the country to hunt and trap during the winter months.

Children and some adults in Rigolet standing near the boxes of toys and Christmas gifts dropped off from the air by personel from the American base in Goose Bay, early 1960s

Children in Rigolet, early 1960s, out to meet the helicopter crew from the American base in Goose Bay, who had just made a Christmas gift drop to them

Our Anglican congregation in North West River was quite small. We used the United Church building for our worship services. The Anglican and United Church people generally worshipped together and supported one another in every way. On my first visit, Mr. Jack Watts asked me where I was going to have the service.

North West River on the far side of the river and Sheshatshiu on the near side. The two communities are divided by the river.

When I replied, "In the United Church," he said, "Good. If you were to have it anywhere else I would not be there." The concentration of Anglicans in North West River was "up the point," where several Montague and Michelin families lived, and from time to time I conducted a service of worship in one or other of their houses. The United Church minister and people were very co-operative and accommodating and would sometimes forgo their Sunday morning service so that the Anglicans could use the church. On a monthly weekend visit to North West River, apart from the times of worship, I visited families at home, patients in the hospital, and dropped in on the school and the residences for out-of-town children.

Mud Lake is just down Hamilton River, east of Happy Valley. My travels there were with whoever would take me along, in speedboat in the summer and snowmobile in the winter. Mud Lake was a small community, a few houses on either side of the Lake with a one-room school and a small United Church. Prior to my being stationed in Happy Valley, the few Anglicans in Mud Lake hadn't seen an Anglican clergyman in years. I first sent word to Aunt Martha Hope—senior ladies in rural Newfoundland communities are frequently accorded the honorary title of Aunt—to say that I was coming over for a visit and to conduct a church service in the United Church. When she received the message she said, "What, who in the world told him about us?"

Overnight in Mud Lake, I always stayed at Aunt Martha's place. It was such a special experience. She slept out of her bed so that I could have the best bed in the house. When I awoke on a Sunday morning I could hear the wood fire crackling and the smell of fried bacon and eggs filled the room. It was so cozy, comfortable, and welcoming. After a hearty breakfast the two of us would trudge off to the United Church with a few others for worship. The United Church organist, Mrs. Maud McLean, was always there to play the organ.

Chris, Carla, and Veronica, about the time Veronica came to live with us in 1965

A few years later, when I made my usual visit to Mud Lake, the speedboat dropped me off on the lakeshore near Aunt Martha's house. I had no sense that anything was wrong and went up over the bank toward her house, only to find her dead on her bridge. It seemed that the dear soul had gotten up in the morning, lit her fire, went outside to look around, and collapsed with a massive heart attack. I was back in Mud Lake a few days later to conduct Aunt Martha's funeral, the celebration of the life of a marvellous person.

In the spring of 1965, a letter from Bishop Meaden informed us that at the request of the Parish of Bay Roberts in Conception Bay, Newfoundland, he would be glad to appoint me as their new rector, effective the first of September. By now we had been in the Mission of Happy Valley (Happy Valley, Mud Lake, North West River, and Rigolet) for eight years and had reached many of the goals set out in 1957. Selma and I felt it was perhaps time to leave and take on some new challenges, so we accepted the appointment.

Just before leaving Happy Valley, Veronica Dyson, at the age of fourteen years, with her parents' consent, came to live with us. While in Happy Valley my immediate family had grown from a solitary one to five. In time we would number seven.

It was difficult to leave the Mission of Happy Valley, more difficult than it was for me to leave Fogo and go off to teachers' college. Selma and I loved the place and the people and felt loved by them. The past eight years had been very formative for me as a priest. I had grown into priesthood with them, my first parish, our first home after marriage, and starting a family. We had been through good times and bad times together. But after the farewells and goodbyes, late in August 1965, Selma, Carla, Christopher, Veronica, and I flew from Goose Bay to St. John's and were escorted to Bay Roberts in Conception Bay by William Crosby and Allan Kelley, who met us at the airport. Our household effects and the Volkswagen would follow on board the *Northern Ranger* in a week to ten days.

North West River, Innu side, where the International Grenfell Association kept their snowmobile. Mode of travel in winter with Ronald Watts.

An Innu man and Aunt Minnie Burry, showing a little of both sides of North West River

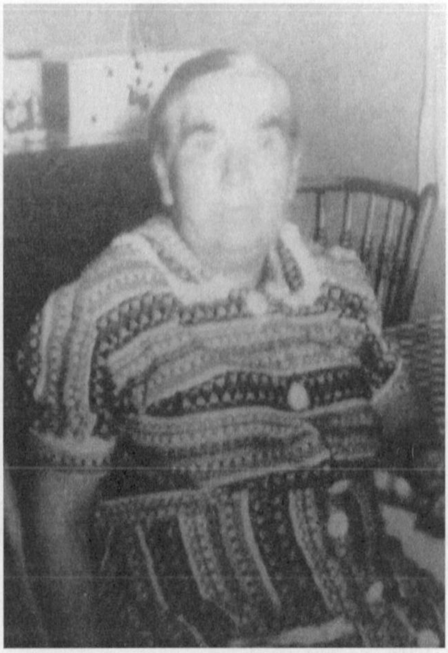

Left: Mode of travel in summer to Mud Lake with Edgar Wolfrey
Right: Aunt Martha Hope, with whom I stayed when visiting Mud Lake

Mud Lake. On the right side is the Reverend Lester Burry's boat, *Glad Tidings*, and the United Church building.

CHAPTER TWELVE
BAY ROBERTS, 1965–1970

In Bay Roberts parish, I was succeeding the Reverend Isaac Butler, who had been our beloved rector in the Parish of Fogo for several years during my boyhood days. He was the priest who had prepared me for confirmation and had involved me as a server and choir member. When Isaac and June (Earle) were married in St. Andrew's Church in Fogo, I pumped the bellows on the church organ for their marriage service. It was not an electric organ then. Now the Butlers had gone to a parish in the Diocese of Nova Scotia and Prince Edward Island.

Moving into a parish just vacated by my former rector could have been a bit intimidating, but on the other hand it was a privilege and honour to follow him. At the time I felt that the eight years' experience in Happy Valley–Goose Bay had well-prepared me for whatever challenges lay ahead.

The Parish of Bay Roberts in those days included Bay Roberts, Coley's Point, Shearstown, and Butlerville. Butlerville, an extension of Shearstown, at one time had its own one-room school but was part of the congregation at St. Mark's Church in Shearstown. It was a long established and traditional parish, so different from the frontier situation in Happy Valley–Goose Bay. All three church buildings—St. Matthew's in Bay Roberts, St. John the Evangelist in Coley's Point, and St. Mark in Shearstown—were only a few minutes' distance from one another. It always takes time to adjust to a new parish situation and it was no different with us, moving from Happy Valley to Bay Roberts. We missed

Happy Valley terribly at first but soon settled in and enjoyed our time in the Parish of Bay Roberts.

Here, patterns and traditions were well set. There were no new buildings to be constructed, no huge responsibilities to be undertaken regarding the school board and school administration. Bay Roberts had an elementary school that was an amalgamated school. The high school, Ascension Collegiate in Bay Roberts, was an Anglican high school serving the five neighbouring parishes: Bay Roberts, South River, Port de Grave, Spaniard's Bay, and Upper Island Cove. Clergy from all five parishes served as members of the school board and assisted with the delivery of the religious education program. The board had a paid staff, a superintendent of education, a secretary treasurer, and maintenance personnel. All this meant that I was much freer to concentrate on pastoral ministry, the building up of the faith community in each of the three congregations, and conduct regular weekly liturgical worship.

On the steps of the rectory in Bay Roberts. Stewart, Robert, Veronica, Selma, Carla, and Christopher.

After eight years in comparative isolation in Labrador, it was great to be in closer contact with neighbouring clergy, but I soon discovered that there were parish boundaries I should not cross. I got myself in trouble on that account a few times. I was on a small committee of the school board that was asked to visit all the schools in the area and check on the work and duties of the janitors. That meant visiting the schools in all five parishes that were run by the one board. It didn't go over well. Some people thought that I should not be going into parishes other than my own. Meanwhile, there was a great deal of sharing and support among the clergy of other denominations in the area, and I soon became acquainted with clergy and people in the United Church and the Salvation Army. We began observing the Week of Prayer for Christian Unity each year in January and worshipped together in one or other of the churches during that week.

Although a parish with a lot of senior citizens, Bay Roberts parish had a lively youth ministry. There was a large company of the Church Lads' Brigade (CLB) that took in lads from other parishes in the area as well. I identified well with the CLB, having grown up with it in Fogo. I attended officers' training in St. John's in order to be more in tune with how things ought to operate. I frequently joined the officers and lads at their weekly assemblies and one summer went to the CLB summer camp in Harbour Grace as their padre. The CLB eventually moved their summer campsite from Harbour Grace to the Mint Brook campsite in Central Newfoundland.

I really enjoyed the summer youth camp experience and went to Mint Brook as padre to one boys' camp directed by my good friend the Reverend David Pearce. David had many gifts that allowed him to excel in ministry to children and young people. He was quite athletic and, in growing up in Burin, was very much involved in soccer, hockey, and basketball. His love of sports carried over and was a great asset in his love of directing summer camps for boys. Although he always liked to win, he taught by example that it is not whether you win or lose but how you play the game.

Sponsored by the Women's Auxiliary, there was an organization for younger girls called the Junior Auxiliary and an organization for older girls called the Girls Auxiliary, as well as a group for baptized children, aged one to five, known as Little Helpers, in each part of the parish. Sunday schools were fairly strong. Girl Guides had been strong previously under the leadership of my predecessor's wife, Mrs. June Butler, and others. With the departure of the Butlers, the Girl Guide Company fell apart, at least for a while. I suspect that the Girls Auxiliary took over some of the work and membership from the Girl Guides. The Anglican Church Women (ACW) was organized in each of the three congregations.

In Coley's Point there was an organization for men known as "The Anglican Church Assistant Association," which was open to men from all over the area. Each of the three churches had good adult choirs and junior choirs. I put a fair amount of time and energy into training servers in each congregation. Servers were people, particularly young people, who assist at church services, doing all sorts of tasks: carrying the Cross, lighting the candles, bringing forward the bread and wine at the Holy Eucharist, and receiving the offering.

At one of my first church services in Coley's Point, an elderly lady said to me as I shook her hand, "I would like a visit sometime soon."

Straightaway, on Monday morning I called on her and discovered that her concern was, "Can I receive Holy Communion?"

This was in the days when a parishioner had to be confirmed or desirous of being confirmed before coming to Holy Communion. I replied, "You are confirmed?"

"Oh, yes, sir," was the reply. "I was confirmed at the age of fourteen but never received Holy Communion because I never felt good enough."

I assured her that she had the same right to receive Holy Communion as me or anyone else, and that if ever we really felt good enough we would be in great danger. At the age of seventy-five years she came to Holy Communion the following Sunday and was a regular communicant thereafter.

Here is another story on the same subject, even more telling. I was paying frequent visits to an elderly parishioner who was near death. He had been a good churchman, had brought up his family in the church, and rarely missed a church service, but he had never received Holy Communion. One afternoon as I was leaving his home I said to his caregiver daughter-in-law, "Do you think Uncle Ray [not his proper name] would like to have Holy Communion?"

She went back into his room and asked him if he would like to have Holy Communion. His answer was, "No."

A few days afterwards, again as I was about to leave his home I said to the daughter-in-law, "Do you think he would like to receive Holy Communion now?"

She replied, "I asked him the last time. You ask him now."

I went back into his room and, speaking gently into his ear, said, "Uncle Ray, would you like to have Holy Communion?"

With a faint, halting voice he answered, "Yes. All our lives we watched other people go and criticized them. That's no good, I want my Communion now."

I had my private Communion set and robe in the car. I brought them in and conducted the Holy Communion service. He received Holy Communion the one and only time in his life, and I could see it meant so very much to him. He died a few days afterwards.

About the time we went to Bay Roberts, the diocese had adopted a policy whereby each parish should pay the cost of heat, light, and telephone at the rectory. To former rectors, the Parish of Bay Roberts had been paying a bonus of $275 a year to cover this. I had informed them that the idea of a bonus was not on anymore but that they should pay the cost of heat, light, and telephone instead. So, at the annual general meetings in February of 1966, they saw for the first time the cost of heat, light, and telephone at the rectory. A heated discussion ensued at the meeting on Coley's Point, and Captain Sam Parsons, whom I hadn't gotten to know well yet, and who afterwards became my churchwarden, said for all to hear, "What do you do over there in the rectory, turn the furnace up top-notch and open all the doors and windows?"

It did hurt, of course, but I explained the policy again and we got on with other business. Those opposed to the policy did eventually see the light.

The Parish of Bay Roberts published a little booklet called *The Challenge*. Printed at Russell's print shop. *The Challenge* contained all the year-end financial statements for the whole parish, the rector's annual letter, and a record of the individual gifts opposite each person's name. It was while we were in the Parish of Bay Roberts that the practice of printing individual gifts was discontinued.

In Shearstown, Eva Bradbury and her husband, Archibald, had had ten children. Arch was now deceased. Eva and her two teenaged children, Helen and Clayton, were living in an old, rundown house that very much needed to be replaced. In St. Mark's congregation we organized ourselves to build a modest new house for Eva and her family. People responded well to our door-to-door collection of money. The Department of Social Services provided some funding. With some paid labour and much free labour we built and furnished a small bungalow adequate for the family of three. Eva was forever grateful to the people of Shearstown and area, and St. Mark's congregation particularly.

Again, as I wrote the previous paragraph and thought about Eva, I contacted our friends Gus and Yvonne Mercer in Shearstown, got Eva's number, and telephoned her. We had a great conversation. She remembered all about our building the house and assured me of her deep gratitude and that she was still comfortably enjoying her special abode. A fall some time ago left her with a broken hip and wrist. She recuperated well and at ninety-three was going strong with the use of a cane and gets out to church still.

In my pastoral visiting in Butlerville, I came upon a young man living under deplorable conditions. The house was dilapidated, dirty, and cold. I was convinced that before the start of another winter he should move in with his sister and her family who lived nearby. His sister was prepared to take him into her home. However, it took a lot of coaxing and some straight talk to convince Lorenzo that he should move. In my attempts to convince him, I invited help from an RCMP officer on one occasion and a doctor on another occasion. One day, in response to my statement that should he stay in this condition during the winter he would likely not survive, he replied, "After all, it is home."

We did finally convince him and he moved in with his sister, much to my relief and the relief of the neighbours, especially his sister.

The range of experiences and emotions that comes in the course of exercising a pastoral ministry are broad and varied. At the time of a death, whatever the age of the person or the circumstances around the death, it is a very difficult time for family and friends. At one time, while we were preparing for the funeral of an elderly parishioner in Bay Roberts, I said to her daughters, "Your mom has been a gift to us for nearly ninety-five years. She has had a good life. We can only be thankful now and look at the funeral liturgy as a celebration of a wonderful life."

Stewart, outside St. Mark's Church in Shearstown, part of Bay Roberts parish

A group of servers gathered at St. Matthew's Church, Bay Roberts. They were from Bay Roberts, Shearstown, and Coley's Point.

Combined church choir from Bay Roberts, Coley's Point, and Shearstown at St. Matthew's Church in Bay Roberts

Junior Auxiliary girls, Girls Auxiliary, and leaders in St. Matthew's Church, Bay Roberts

One of the daughters turned to me and said, “Yes sir, I know that what you are saying is true, but she is still our mother.” I’ve never forgotten that.

While we were still in Bay Roberts, Bishop Seaborn appointed me his junior examining chaplain. The Reverend Percy Clarke, one of the teaching staff at Queen’s College, was the bishop’s examining chaplain. Percy and I worked together preparing transitional deacons for their ordination as priests. We administered a form of examination and provided an opportunity for a quiet retreat prior to ordination.

Bay Roberts was the sort of parish where one could get comfortable and stay on for too long a time. I was far too young, thirty-eight years old at the time, and had no intention of staying too long. In the meantime, Bishop Meaden had retired, and Bishop Robert Seaborn, the assistant bishop in Newfoundland, succeeded Bishop Meaden as diocesan bishop on February 2, 1966. In the spring of 1970, Bishop Seaborn dropped by one afternoon on his way home to St. John’s, just for a friendly visit, to see how we were doing, and to have a cup of tea. He mentioned the fact that there were several parishes on the Northern Peninsula needing priests, particularly Flower’s Cove and St. Anthony. I made it clear to him that, as much as we loved being in Bay Roberts and felt that we were having a good ministry, I was available to go when and where he wanted me to go. He thanked me and said he would keep that in mind. A few weeks later, I received a telephone call from Bishop Seaborn asking if I would consider going to Flower’s Cove parish or St. Anthony parish. Selma and I thought about it, and because of our ties to St. Anthony, it being her birthplace, where she still had family, we decided in favour of the ten-point (ten small communities with congregations) Mission of St. Anthony. Bishop Seaborn was pleased to make the appointment effective September 1, 1970.

Some of our dear folks in Bay Roberts couldn’t believe that we were going north again. A neighbour said, “I could understand it if you were moving to St. John’s, but I can’t understand why you’re going north again after coming from Goose Bay only five years ago.” To some it seemed like a demotion, and perhaps it was, but not to us.

This is where the need was greatest at that time, and we were up to the challenge.

We were quite attached to the folks in Bay Roberts parish. It was difficult to pull away. But farewell events over and goodbyes said, we took our leave at the end of August with heavy hearts at leaving Veronica behind in St. John's, at the Grace Hospital School of Nursing. She would go back to her family in Happy Valley for the summer and would return to the Grace Hospital in St. John's in September. We kept wondering how she would make out, another year with us so far away.

On our way driving up through Bay Roberts, I decided to stop and say a final farewell to my friend Captain Sam Parsons. On leaving his house he said, "Sir, I'm glad you stopped because there is something I've been meaning to tell you for a long time. I am terribly sorry for what I said to you at that first annual meeting at Coley's Point about heat, light, and telephone costs at the rectory. I've never been so sorry about anything in my life. I should have known better. Forgive me."

My reply was, "There is nothing to forgive. It was all part of doing the church's business at an annual general meeting. I fully understand. You are a good parishioner and you were a good churchwarden while I was in the parish. All the best to you and your family."

CHAPTER THIRTEEN
ST. ANTHONY, 1970–1978

In 1970, the Mission of St. Anthony covered ten different communities, ten different congregations: St. Anthony, Big Brook, Boat Harbour, Cook's Harbour including "The Bight," Raleigh, Griquet, Noddy Bay, Quirpon, L'Anse aux Meadows, and St. Carol's.

By 1970, all the communities in the parish were connected by road, except for St. Carol's. A visit to St. Carol's could be by boat from St. Anthony Bight or overland. For my first visit I contacted Uncle Harry Richards in St. Carol's, and he came by speedboat to St. Anthony Bight and picked me up. On the way to St. Carol's, the engine failed, and we drifted for some time in the wrong direction. Until the road went through to St. Carol's soon afterwards, I chose to go the way of a thirty-minute walk over the hills from St. Anthony Bight to St. Carol's and to hop on a skidoo with someone in the winter.

There were three church buildings in the parish: the new St. Mary's in St. Anthony (first service held Christmas Eve, 1969, and dedicated in June 1970), St. Matthew's in Cook's Harbour, and St. Peter's (not in use anymore) in Quirpon. I learned that St. Peter's in Quirpon was built many years earlier largely by the initiative, resources, and help from the fisherfolk who came to the area from other parts of Newfoundland for the summer fishery and was used for worship mainly in the summer when fisherfolk were around. In 1970, the fisherfolk were long gone and, with only two Anglican families in Quirpon, the unused St. Peter's Church building was in a sad state of disrepair. Church services were being held now in the home of Frank and Stella Elms.

William Gordon Legge was consecrated a bishop in the Cathedral Church of St. John the Baptist in St. John's January 25, 1968, and commissioned by the bishop of Newfoundland, Bishop Robert Seaborn, in St. John the Evangelist Church in Corner Brook May 4, 1968, as the assistant bishop of the Diocese of Newfoundland. On one of his visits to the Parish of St. Anthony, Bishop Legge deconsecrated St. Peter's Church in Quirpon. The old building was later sold for a small sum of money to a family who intended to use the materials to build a house. In Boat Harbour, Raleigh, and St. Carol's the schools and school chapels were used for worship. Noddy Bay, Big Brook, and Quirpon had house churches. I would do services in the house churches on a weekday evening and try to cover the other seven congregations on alternate Sundays. Sunday services were held every Sunday 9:00 a.m., 11:00 a.m., 3:00 p.m., and 7:00 p.m. I tried to be as fair as possible and give everyone equal time and opportunity for assembly and worship, realizing that the larger numbers in some congregations needed more time by way of pastoral care and worship. Lay leadership in the conduct of church services was on the rise and made the schedule of services more possible. When I was leading worship in one part of the parish, a lay reader would lead morning or evening prayer in another part of the parish.

Of the few families in Big Brook, two were Anglican, Bill Bailey's family and Uncle Ben McLean's family. Uncle Ben was quite elderly and had his own ideas about how often the parson should visit and hold services. On at least one occasion when I hadn't measured up to his standard, he reported me to Bishop Seaborn. I learned in time that I wasn't the first priest that he complained about to the bishop, bless his heart.

The work in the far-flung Parish of St. Anthony and the distance from St. John's and Queen's College precluded my continuing to act as the bishop's junior examining chaplain. In the meantime, Bishop Seaborn wrote me in November 1970 to say that the division of the Humber–St. Barbe deanery had been approved and that he was appointing me as rural dean of the new St. Barbe deanery. This new deanery would take in all the parishes on the Northern Peninsula, from Bonne Bay north to St. Anthony and the Parish of Forteau in southern Labrador. The duties of a regional dean were not thought to be onerous in those days. If a parish in the deanery was without a priest for a period of time, the regional dean arranged to have emergencies and the sacramental aspects of ministry looked after. Bishop Seaborn's concern was that the clergy should meet together from time to time, pray together, and support one another.

It was obvious that the Mission of St. Anthony was near the time when we should seek parish status. We seemed to be doing fairly well financially. Certainly we ought to be able at this point to do without the grant-in-aid from the Diocese of Newfoundland. We contacted synod office to that effect and in 1971 the Mission of St. Anthony became the self-supporting Parish of St. Anthony.

The Reverend Cyrus Pitman, rector of the neighbouring Parish of Flower's Cove (later bishop of Eastern Newfoundland and Labrador), and I took in the supervised pastoral education (SPE) offered at the Nova Scotia Sanitarium, Kentville, NS, June 26 to August 5, 1972. Iliffe Sheppard, a theology student, filled in as student minister in the Parish of St. Anthony while I was away.

In September of 1972, I had the very great pleasure of going back to Happy Valley–Goose Bay for a few days to celebrate with St. Andrew's congregation the consecration of St. Andrew's Church. Thirteen years earlier, while I was their priest, St. Andrew's was built. Now debt free, it was consecrated by Bishop Robert Seaborn on September 17, 1972. It was a real homecoming for me. It was so good to see former parishioners again and share in the special event. Among the visiting clergy who attended the special event was the Reverend Canon Felix Honeygold, rector of St. Michael and All Angels parish in St. John's. Many years previously, Canon Felix Honeygold was the priest in charge of the Mission of Sandwich Bay and was the first priest to make periodic visits to the new community of Happy Valley.

The new St. Mary's Church in St. Anthony had only been in use a few months before I became the new rector in September of 1970.

To build the new church, the congregation had acquired a fairly large debt in the form of a bank loan. The interior of the church basement had to be completed so that we could use it as a parish hall. We took on this project right away. The response to the call for free labour was tremendous. Each vestry member took a list of people to contact for a specific night's work. As a result, there were nights when so many people turned up that some of them couldn't find work to do and went home again. This was the case in spite of the fact that, even then, there was a feeling that the days of free labour were over. It just needed to be organized and people needed to be asked personally. In a short time the parish hall was completed and in use.

To pay down the bank loan as quickly as possible and save on interest payments meant a constant round of special collections, fundraisers, and letters to parishioners keeping them up-to-date, thanking them and encouraging them to keep up the good work. The congregation was very responsive and generous. As a result the new St. Mary's was debt free and consecrated by Bishop W. Gordon Legge in November 1975.

Previous to having a fine parish hall, the Sunday school met each Sunday afternoon in St. Mary's School down on the east side of St. Anthony. Because of my schedule of church services, I couldn't participate and support the work of the Sunday school as I would like. With the completion of the parish hall we started having Sunday school around the Sunday morning 11:00 a.m. service. The enrolment greatly increased to the point where we couldn't accommodate them all at one time in the parish hall. One half of the Sunday school children and their teachers had to stay upstairs while the other half attended Sunday school in the hall, and halfway through the church service we switched; the ones in the hall came up to the church service, while the ones upstairs went down to the hall for their Sunday school session.

To be part of the Sunday school ministry, I tried to be in St. Mary's Church in St. Anthony more often for the 11:00 a.m. Sunday morning worship, while doing services in the outlying places at 9:00 a.m., 3:00 p.m., and 7:00 p.m. It made for a tight schedule. Leading a nine o'clock service in Griquet, for example, barely gave me enough time to get back to St. Anthony for the eleven o'clock service. I couldn't afford to have a flat tire or any other delay. I would be late for sure.

Meanwhile, the old St. Mary's Church on Murray's Point, in St. Anthony, was becoming more and more dilapidated. It had been deconsecrated for some time. Title to the old property was being disputed by one person, claiming that when the church didn't need the land for church purposes anymore it was to revert to the estate of the person who gave the land in the first place (his father). A trip to the Crown lands office in St. John's settled that matter. The land had been deeded to the church with no strings attached. Finally, the old property was sold to Truman Mitchelmore, who intended to salvage some of the materials for use in the building of a house. Then, while Truman was working in Goose Bay, one Guy Fawkes' Night (November 5), some young people, needing bonfire materials, set the old church building afire. The fire was quickly extinguished by the St. Anthony volunteer fire brigade. A week or two before Guy Fawkes' Night rolled around again, I saw to it, with Truman's consent, that the old building was destroyed by controlled burning. Interestingly, one person who suspected the fire to be another act of vandalism remarked, "Reverend Payne will be so upset." Little did they know at the time that I was behind it all. I couldn't have been happier with the outcome.

The time had come to replace the old rectory on the east side of St. Anthony with a new one near the new St. Mary's Church. I once heard that the old rectory was originally Dr. Wilfred Grenfell's summer house. In the autumn of 1972, with the help of a "Canada Works Program," we started to build the new rectory. We managed to get the basement poured and the house covered in before the start of winter. In February 1973, the old rectory, on the east side of St. Anthony, was totally destroyed by fire. The cause of the fire, it seems, was an electrical malfunction in the upstairs area. The fire spread quickly. Thanks to the volunteer fire brigade, the fire was brought under control, but the house was a writeoff. We lost practically everything upstairs but salvaged most of our possessions on the main floor. More will be said about the fire in the chapter "Our Family."

All church properties were insured through the diocesan office in St. John's, but not always for replacement value. The irony was that just weeks before the fire I had brought the matter of insurance to the parish council and the decision was to increase the coverage on the rectory to $15,000, still nowhere near replacement value. When I telephoned the synod office in St. John's to report the fire, I was told that we did indeed have $15,000 coverage, only recently added. Bishop Seaborn said to me, "Stewart, if I didn't know you so well, I would have to think this was planned."

One spring in the mid-1970s, a group of Greenpeace people came to St. Anthony just as our men were about to prosecute the seal fishery. They came with the intent of going out on the ice, daubing green paint on some whitecoat seals to spoil the pelts, and preventing the seal fishery from going ahead. The evening before they were to go out on the ice, a public meeting was held in the auditorium of Harriett Curtis Collegiate. The Greenpeace people were present as well as many of the fishermen and their families. I was asked to speak on behalf of the clergy in the area and their people. I kept a copy of what I said that night. Here it is:

"Mr. Chairman, ladies and gentlemen, I have been appointed the local church representative to speak on behalf of the clergy and their church people at this meeting, in defence of the seal fishing industry. I hasten to add that, as clergy, we represent our people: we are not here to represent government or because government officials asked us but because we want to make sure that our people have a voice in this matter. A person said to me yesterday that he didn't think the churches should be involved. Well, the church is people and, since people are involved, the church is involved. There comes a time when we can no longer be silent but must speak our minds, show our concerns, and state our positions.

"This task sounds much easier than it really is. When we stop to think of all the involvement, all the different groups and individuals, some for and some against the seal fishery, and all the motives and reasons for their interests, it becomes a very involved and complicated affair. I do not wish to give the impression that it is simple and that there are easy answers.

"God is the Creator of all. He has entrusted to mankind, who is the highest order of being on earth, the management and control of many things, including the birds of the air and the fish of the sea. Mankind has a great responsibility to manage well and use properly what God has entrusted to us, not to misuse or abuse it. That is a very fundamental principle which the church upholds and teaches continually.

"Killing seals for the meat and the pelts has gone on in coastal Newfoundland and Labrador ever since people have been living here. Mind you, we don't eat seal meat only. Here and everywhere people kill cows, lambs, and pigs for meat. They trap rabbits and shoot moose and caribou for meat, too. Newfoundlanders, in the main, have been as considerate and humane as any other people in providing for their families. Nobody enjoys killing animals. We have never done it just for the sake of doing it, never just for sport, but always for a livelihood.

"The seal fishery is an industry in Newfoundland and Labrador, a very real part of our livelihood and economy. Without emotion, I can tell you what it meant to me in my growing up on Fogo Island in Notre Dame Bay. Meat and a lot of other things were scarce in the spring of the year. The only store-bought meat we had for the most part was salt beef, and that was often scarce in the spring of the year. A few seals, this time of year, meant almost the difference between life and death for many people. We never thought for a second that there was any inhumaneness attached to it. What we did know was that men risked their lives and some lost their lives harvesting seals for their families' food and well-being. Our men dragged to shore all the carcasses as well as the pelts. This was hard work and time-consuming. A change of wind which carried the ice off shore meant that some men never made it back to shore. There was loss of life almost every spring.

"Nothing was left on the ice and nothing was wasted. The meat was shared around to friends and neighbours who couldn't prosecute the seal fishery. The skins were normally sold, but not all. Some were kept and made into much-needed boots [skin boots], mittens, and other items of clothing right here at home. It doesn't mean quite as much today, perhaps, but it meant a great deal some years ago. One of the fundraising endeavours, initiated and led by the rector of Flower's Cove parish, Reverend Canon Richards, of blessed memory, for the building of St. Barnabas's Church in Flower's Cove, Strait of Belle Isle, was the sale of sealskin boots, which the women of Flower's Cove made for that purpose. That church has been referred to as the 'Skin Boot Church.'

"The seal fishery is an industry. The church asks people to prosecute it with responsibility and humaneness. I am not a scientist. I don't know if the seal is an endangered species or not. Our federal and provincial governments should know this after doing researches and surveys. We have to look to them for guidance and direction in this respect. I hear conflicting stories. Some say it is an endangered species and produce figures to prove it, others produce figures to prove the very opposite. This matter cannot be resolved in St. Anthony or on the icefields but by mutual study and research on a higher, governmental plane.

"Greenpeace people, you are putting the people of this area in a difficult position. You are giving us a bad name, a name we don't deserve. On a positive note in closing, by being here you may understand our culture and our people better and give more thought to the course of action you propose. Thank you, thank you very much."

After that meeting I invited the Greenpeace people to the rectory, my home, for a cup of tea. Some of them were able to come along and we had a great conversation about the seal fishery and other matters. I'm not sure what happened the next day. They may have gone out on the ice, but I doubt that they would have gotten near many whitecoat seals. I don't recall a troubling incident between them and the fishermen.

I will always remember one winter deanery meeting in Cow Head in the midst of a snowstorm. The meeting concluded but the roads, blocked with snow, delayed our departure from Cow Head. On Saturday we heard that the Northern Peninsula Highway was open except for a section, the five or six miles from Big Brook to Cook's Harbour. We left Cow Head to return to our homes. I dropped Cyrus Pitman off in Flower's Cove. He and Mary thought that I should hold up with them until I was sure that the road between Big Brook and

Cook's Harbour was open, but I pressed on, thinking that by the time I got that far the road would certainly be open. I came up behind the snowblower in the Big Brook area and realized that the road was still blocked. What I didn't know was that the snowblower on the opposite end had broken down and had gone back to Cook's Harbour. In one narrow cut a little wider than the car, walls of snow on either side, there was no way I could turn around and go back to Flower's Cove.

As the snowblower operator, Wilga White, cleared a few more yards, the vehicles following would move up behind him and stop. So, it went on all through the night. From time to time Wilga would stop the machine, lean over the wheel, and rest for a few minutes. It was eerie to stand outside the car from time to time and experience the dead silence, except for the noise of the snowblower, and wonder how we would fare should we ever be stuck in this snow tunnel by another storm. As daylight began to break, around 6:00 a.m., Wilga stopped the machine, came back to my car with his lunch box in his hand, and offered me a share of his lunch. I refused at first, saying that he was the one who had been working hard all night while I rested, and that he needed all the food he had there. He insisted, so I took a little of his lunch.

By ten o'clock Sunday morning Wilga's job of opening that stretch of highway was complete. From here on the road was open to St. Anthony. One cut, at least. I knew my Sunday schedule of services: I should be in Raleigh for the 11:00 a.m. worship service, so off to Raleigh I went. As I waited for the small congregation to assemble, I discovered that the Gospel reading for the day was the story how Jesus fed the multitude with the lad's gift of loaves and fishes. I was able to work into my sermon the story how Wilga, tired and weary after operating the snowblower all through the night, came to me at morning light and gladly shared his lunch, not a miracle in the way most people think of miracles, but certainly a heartwarming moment.

Out of interest, as I was writing this story, approximately forty years afterwards, I felt the need to check on Wilga White in Sandy Cove, near Flower's Cove. I telephoned him and we had a great conversation. He remembered the story well, every detail of it. His wife has since died. He lives alone in Sandy Cove but spends the winters with his daughters in Ontario. Stories such as this one have given me an insight into the calibre of the people who serve the public, day and night, often in stormy and hazardous conditions, keeping our highways clear and safe in winter.

One year, early in April, during my tenure in St. Anthony parish, the Reverend Cyrus Pitman, rector of Flower's Cove parish, and I decided to do a pulpit exchange on Good Friday. The unpaved highway, at that time of year with melting snow and ice, was full of ice-rimmed potholes, a sure weapon to rubber tires. The day went well for both of us. On the way back from Flower's Cove I was to stop in Cook's Harbour for an evening church service. Five or six miles short of Cook's Harbour I fell victim to a large, icy pothole and punctured my gas tank. My gas tank registered empty as I parked by St. Matthew's Church in Cook's Harbour. Before starting the church service, I shared my troubles with Roy Pittman, a mechanic with the Department of Highways. When I came out of church after the service, my car was still parked by the church. I soon discovered that, while we were inside, Roy had taken my car to the Highways garage, repaired the damaged tank, added some gas, and parked it back by the church. After checking in with Roy and thanking him, I was able to finish my day at home in St. Anthony. Again, it speaks volumes about the calibre of people who go far beyond the call of duty to help another person.

During my winters in St. Anthony, I came to have a great respect for all the highway workers who worked tirelessly, in good weather and in bad weather, to keep our roads open and all travellers safe. I remember so well the admonition of Ralph Pittman, the Highways foreman, when I was leaving Cook's Harbour for St. Anthony in threatening winter weather: "Go on, if you come upon snowdrifts down the bay, just stop, don't try to drive through. We will be down there shortly and rescue you." And it always worked out that way. They were all so responsible, dependable, and helpful. Nothing was too much trouble for those unsung heroes. Many, many thanks.

At every opportunity I tried to inform families about Killdevil Camp in Gros Morne National Park, near Lomond in Bonne Bay, and the ministry provided there through summer camps for boys and girls of all ages. One summer I was the director of a boys' camp at Killdevil. Several summers Selma and I were on the staff of the junior girls' camp with Sadie Dredge as camp director. Sadie (Clarke) Dredge grew up in Lomond. She raised her family in Corner Brook and has lived there ever since. Selma was one of the camp moms and answered to the name "Polly." Sadie was always "Sparkle." I was simply "Padre."

In May of 1975, the International Grenfell Association (IGA) board elected me to be a director-at-large of the Association. I gladly accepted the invitation to serve and continued to do so for the remaining years of our stay in St. Anthony. These were the days before local, regional health boards in Northern Newfoundland and Labrador. Dr. Gordon Thomas was then executive director of the IGA. The IGA board meetings were held twice a year, once in New York and once in Boston, because that was where there were a number of local organizations raising funds for the work of the IGA. England and Canada, too, had some local IGA fundraising organizations. The IGA board members came from England, the United States of America, and Canada. I have no idea when the IGA began to receive financial assistance from the Newfoundland Government. It was a tremendous privilege and joy to be a member of the IGA board and associated with the great work begun by Dr. Wilfred Grenfell, the mission's founder.

I attended the IGA meetings in Boston and New York each year from 1975 to 1978.

On the flight back to St. John's from one of those meetings late in December, while the plane was on the ground in Halifax, we were allowed off the plane for a short time. I made my way into the terminal and into a small bookstore. Time passed quickly, and when I didn't hear a call to board the plane again I went up to the ticket counter, only to be told that the plane was already in the air and there would not be another flight until midday the next day. That meant that I would miss my connecting IGA plane from St. John's to St. Anthony and be delayed in St. John's for several days. You can imagine my anxiety and embarrassment, having to report the matter at home, call a friend in Halifax to rescue me for the night, and to be absent from church services on Sunday.

Youth delegates at the synod in St. Anthony, 1977

The synod members gathered for worship at St. Mary's Church, St. Anthony, 1977

In the spring of 1977, the Parish of St. Anthony hosted the annual synod, an assembly of the bishop, clergy, and lay representatives in the Diocese of Western Newfoundland, in St. Anthony, the first synod to be held outside the City of Corner Brook. Parishioners accommodated the delegates in their homes. Almost every family had to take in one or two delegates. The synod meetings were held in the auditorium of Harriett Curtis Collegiate. The noonday and evening meals were served in St. Mary's Parish Hall by the Anglican Church Women of the parish.

Little did we know at the time that, a year from then, at a special synod in Corner Brook, I would be elected as bishop coadjutor (a coadjutor bishop is one who automatically succeeds as diocesan bishop without further election) to succeed Bishop Legge as diocesan bishop. My family and I would have to move to Corner Brook, thus ending eight years as rector of the Parish of St. Anthony.

CHAPTER FOURTEEN
CORNER BROOK, AND A SPECIAL VISIT TO FOGO

Through the process of restructuring, Western Newfoundland became an autonomous diocese in 1976. Corner Brook became the See city, the centre from where the bishop exercises oversight and jurisdiction. The Church of St. John the Evangelist became the Pro Cathedral, the temporary designation prior to determining whether it was the right choice for the designation "Cathedral." There were nineteen parishes in the Diocese of Western Newfoundland. Space for the diocesan synod office was rented in the Millbrook Mall in Corner Brook. Mrs. Jean Clarke became the office manager and the bishop's secretary.

In 1977, Bishop Gordon Legge announced that he would retire as bishop of the Diocese of Western Newfoundland at the end of July 1978. The date for a special synod to elect his successor was set for April 14, 1978, in Corner Brook.

My name kept coming up as a possible candidate. People kept assuring me that I would be the next bishop of Western Newfoundland, so much so that I had to give it some thought and prayerful consideration. Was there a possibility that I might be elected? What if I were? The thought of being a bishop was overwhelming. How could I ever fulfill that awesome role? Some months before the electoral synod I was approached by the Reverend Charles Abraham, spokesperson for the people, seeking permission to nominate me in advance.

It was in keeping with the diocesan constitution to nominate candidates in advance of the synod, while the first ballot would be a nominating ballot anyway. Quite a few names would come up on the first ballot and, along with those nominated already, would be the list from which to choose a new bishop. I expressed my feeling that we should wait and see; if my name came up on the first ballot, so be it. But finally my answer to Charles was, "It won't make much difference one way or another. If you want to nominate me in advance, go ahead, I'm fine with that."

Synod delegates, twenty-eight clergy and ninety-five lay delegates, gathered at the St. John the Evangelist Church in Corner Brook for the opening of the electoral synod on Thursday evening, April 13, 1978. In attendance also were Clyde Wells, our diocesan chancellor, Bishop Reginald Hollis of Montreal, Bishop Gordon Legge, and Archbishop Robert Seaborn of Eastern Newfoundland and Labrador, president of the synod.

I spent the night with my host family, William and Betty Boyd, formerly of St. Anthony. I never sleep well the first night in a new bed, but it was the business of the next day that excluded some hours of sleep that night.

The next morning, April 14, the electoral synod was called to order to elect Bishop Legge's successor. Archbishop Robert Seaborn presided. Bishop Reginald Hollis gave a number of inspiring devotional addresses while the ballots were being counted. Two candidates, the Reverend Owen Coffin, rector of the Parish of Port aux Basques, and I were nominated beforehand. Several other names appeared on the first ballot, but from start to finish it was mainly a race between Owen and me. Bishop Hollis's deeply devotional addresses gave everyone the sense of quiet confidence that the synod, conducted in an atmosphere of prayer, was under the guidance of God the Holy Spirit, and whatever the outcome, it should be seen as electing the one called by God.

After several ballots I was declared elected to succeed Bishop Gordon Legge. I accepted the election, believing deep within that it was a call from God and the Diocese of Western Newfoundland, and trusted in the ongoing help, guidance, and support of God the Holy Spirit. As soon as I could, I telephoned Selma. There were more tears than words. In her modest, gentle, and selfless way she said, "It is no surprise to me. Remember, I told you so."

Bishop Legge invited several of the synod delegates to Bishop's Lodge on Cobb Lane that evening for a time of fellowship and sharing. Among them was the Reverend Lloyd Collett, who always had a story or joke to tell. Reflecting on the special synod and the election, he said without a smile, "Now we don't have a Legge to stand on and we are all in a Stew."

As soon as the news of my election spread, and in the time leading up to my ordination as bishop, telegrams, cards, and letters came in from family, friends, and parishioners attesting very kindly to our relationships and my ministry over the years as a priest, and expressing every confidence in my ability to lead in the Diocese of Western Newfoundland. I was deeply touched by the warmth of the greetings and good wishes and acknowledged each one, with gratitude, in a handwritten note. I would like to share this one brief letter with you. It was from Bishop Vicars Short, bishop of Saskatchewan.

> My dear Bishop elect,
>
> Congratulations and felicitations upon your election to the See of Western Newfoundland. May your episcopate be long, fruitful and joyful. I shall avoid giving you advice (tempting though such an exercise is) and content myself by reminding you that one thing only is needful, and that is that you be found faithful.
>
> I shall look forward to seeing you at Lambeth. You are remembered in my prayers. With every blessing.
>
> Yours sincerely,
> Vicars, Bishop of Saskatchewan

That letter, more than any other, has meant so much to me. Over the years I have recalled it and reflected on it again and again. "One thing only is needful, and that is that you be found faithful." I made it the subject of one of my first sermons after becoming a bishop. I soon learned that the demands and expectations on any bishop are daunting, and that Bishop Vicars Short was right: They can only be met and satisfied to any degree through being faithful—faithful to God, faithful to Jesus the Christ, faithful to the church, faithful to oneself, and faithful to others. The same is required of all God's people, not just the bishops. It is one thing to have faith, it is another thing to be faithful. There is a difference. Like the rest of us, I have endeavoured to be faithful, by God's help.

The date for my ordination as bishop was set for June 23, 1978, the eve of St. John the Baptist Day. In preparation, I had now to acquire, among other things, bishop's robes, a pectoral Cross, and a ring. I was directed and sent off to Toronto to "Dorothy Shuter Robes" to be measured for the appropriate bishop's robes. The primate—first among bishops and, in this case, head of the Anglican Church in Canada—of the day, Archbishop Ted Scott, very kindly took me to stay with him and his wife, Isabelle, and assisted me in doing what had to be done. Measurements were duly taken. I picked up a modest ring at a pawnshop for $10. Archbishop Scott gave me an amethyst stone to be set in the ring. Back home in St. Anthony, Mr. Eli Canning, one of the Grenfell Mission carvers in the industrial-handicraft centre, made my pectoral Cross free of charge.

I would like to tell you what eventually happened to that Cross. In the course of one of my visits to the rectory in Burgeo, when the Reverend Glenn Small, his wife, Shirley, and their boys Michael, David, and Ryan were there, David took a fancy to my pectoral Cross and asked me to give it to him. In response to David's repeated requests I said, "I can't give you my Cross now, but when I retire you can have it." Retirement would not be a consideration for many more years, but David never forgot the promise. After nearly twenty years as diocesan bishop and beginning my retirement, the call came from David's father, Glenn: "David wants the Cross you promised him."

I packed up the Cross, which I treasured dearly, and sent it off to David Small. David and his family live in Corner Brook now. Whenever we meet, that Cross is the subject of conversation, and I am assured that it is treasured and being kept safe.

To afford me some quiet, reflective time—a retreat—leading up to my ordination, the metropolitan, Archbishop Seaborn, arranged for

Bishop Timothy Matthews, retired bishop of the Diocese of Quebec, to spend some time with me in St. Anthony. It wasn't a structured retreat as such. We caught whatever time we could, and in Dr. Fitzgerald's home, where Bishop Tim was staying, we reflected on the life and work of a bishop in the Church of God. Bishop Tim didn't give formal addresses but spoke from meaningful experiences in his own life and episcopate. I still remember some of his sayings. "When you don't have time to pray, then you really need to pray," and, speaking of clergy-bishop relationships, "If one can be unfaithful with you, one can be unfaithful to you."

For the ordination service, there was some concern about the seating capacity of St. John the Evangelist Church. Bishop R. T. McGrath, bishop of the Roman Catholic Diocese of St. George's, offered Bishop Legge the use of the Roman Catholic Cathedral, on Mt. Bernard Avenue in Corner Brook, with a greater seating capacity than that of St. John the Evangelist Church. I gladly and gratefully agreed. On June 23, 1978, the eve of St. John the Baptist Day, I was ordained a bishop in the Church of God, in the Roman Catholic Cathedral in Corner Brook, filled to capacity with an estimated 1,100 people from all over the diocese and beyond, including ten bishops from dioceses in Eastern Canada and representatives from other denominations and organizations.

Being ordained a deacon in 1957 and a priest in 1958 were momentous occasions, the consecration as bishop even more so, if that were possible. I knew the gravity of the promises I was making and the enormity of the responsibilities of the office of bishop.

Over the years I have often gone back to the Book of Common Prayer ordination service and reflected on the promises I made on that day. Just to give a snapshot, in the examination part of the service I answered that I was persuaded that I was truly called according to the will of Our Lord Jesus Christ and the order of this Church, and promised to be faithful in guarding the faith, unity, and discipline of the Church; to ordain others, and send them out; to be in all things an example of good works unto others; to maintain and set forward quietness, peace, gentleness, and love among all. Also to be faithful in prayer, and the study of Holy Scripture, and to be merciful to all, showing compassion to the poor, and needy, and all strangers destitute of help.

Left to right: Selma, Isabel Scott, Archbishop Ted Scott (primate of the Anglican Church of Canada), and Stewart. Following my election, I stayed with Ted and Isabel on my visit to Toronto to be measured for bishop's robes. Taken in front of the Bishop's Residence in Corner Brook.

The bishops of the Ecclesiastical Province of Canada about to lay hands on the bishop-elect, Stewart, June 23, 1978

The investiture, a presentation of the symbols of the office of a bishop, followed the laying on of hands by all the bishops present. The most moving part of the investiture was when our four children—Carla, Christopher, Robert, and Angela—came forward with the pectoral Cross and, as Angela placed the Cross around my neck, said those words together, "May this emblem of our redemption rest always upon your heart and speak to you of gain through loss, of triumph through suffering, of life through death, and may the love of the crucified sustain and uphold you." I was deeply, deeply moved. I am sustained in the hope and trust that I have been "found faithful."

The investiture, with all four children standing there and Angela putting the pectoral Cross around my neck

Archbishop Seaborn and the diocesan bishops presented me to the people, saying, "We present to you, Stewart, our brother bishop in the Church of God." When the applause died down I responded with the peace. "The peace of the Lord be always with you." The people responded, "And also with you." Following the sharing of the peace, the service continued with the Holy Eucharist. A public reception followed at the parish hall, in the basement of St. John the Evangelist Pro Cathedral.

FOGO

To give back, a little, to St. Andrew's congregation in Fogo, who had played such a big part in my faith formation and nurture, the Reverend Leonard Ludlow, one-time rector of St. Augustine's Church in St. John's but originally from Fogo, in consultation with Mr. George Oake of Fogo and many of the clergy who grew up on Fogo Island, planned a gathering for worship and thanksgiving in St. Andrew's Church the following Sunday, June 25. I will never forget the feeling as I drove into the community from the Fogo Island ferry to see the flags flying and a big bell arch at the entrance to St. Andrew's Church, with a sign in big, bold letters atop the arch: "WELCOME TO OUR BISHOP." I parked the car and went into the church alone. It was an emotional time, with all the memories of my association with this church flooding back as I knelt there quietly in a reflective mood.

St. Andrew's congregation, Fogo, leaving the church after the special service of Thanksgiving, Sunday, June 25, 1978

I presided at the special service on Sunday, Leonard Ludlow preached a stirring sermon, and all the clergy present shared in leading the worship. A reception followed in the parish hall, which gave me the opportunity to meet, greet, and say a big thank you to St. Andrew's parishioners.

From Fogo, my family and I returned to Corner Brook, where I attended a synod executive meeting chaired by Bishop Legge. The next day we left for St. Anthony, where I would finish off my work and coordinate the move of our belongings to the Bishop's Residence in Corner Brook. We had to go through Woody Point, Bonne Bay, to take the car ferry to Norris Point. While there I made a telephone call to St. Anthony, only to hear the terrible news from Dr. Trudy O'Keefe that a car had gone over the community wharf an hour or so before, into St. Anthony harbour, with five teenagers on board. Austin Hillier managed to free himself and get to shore, but the other four did not. Lindsay Rumbolt, the driver, and three young women—Ivy Way, Pansy Keats, and Sharon Keats—drowned. We hurried on to St. Anthony and I spent the next few days with the grieving families and relatives and making funeral arrangements. Ivy Way was from Savage Cove, in the Strait of Belle Isle, and her body was taken home for burial. I conducted the one funeral service at St. Mary's Church for the other three victims: Lindsay, Pansy, and Sharon. I could never give expression in words to those difficult, difficult days. While writing about this tragic event, I telephoned Florence Keats, mother of Pansy; Mabel Keats, mother of Sharon; and Lindsay's sister Lillian, just to keep in touch, and to know that they were comfortable with my writing about the tragedy. It is so special to reconnect with people I have known so well, and under particular circumstances in pastoral ministry, and assure them of my love and prayers.

We had come to prepare for leaving St. Anthony for Corner Brook, but we were not leaving St. Anthony, really. It was a parish in the Diocese of Western Newfoundland and I would have oversight as diocesan bishop and be visiting St. Anthony parish from time to time. Besides that, Selma's dad and some family members were there, whom we would certainly visit on occasion. With farewell events over and goodbyes said, we took our leave.

A. H. Murray and Company had a couple of large trucks travelling empty from St. Anthony to Corner Brook, and Mr. Nath Chaytor, the company's manager, kindly offered to load the trucks with our household goods and take them to Corner Brook. Bishop and Mrs. Legge had vacated the Bishop's Residence at 13 Cobb Lane, Corner Brook, and had gone to their cottage in Portland, Bonavista Bay, for the summer, while the diocesan retirement home was being built on Glenhaven Boulevard in Corner Brook. The Bishop's Residence was not ready for us to move in, so we simply deposited our household effects there with the help of a group of friends and neighbours. In the meantime, John and Sadie Dredge, who were staying at their cottage in Pasadena Beach, let us occupy their house in Corner Brook for the few days before I was required to be off to England for the 1978 Lambeth conference.

CHAPTER FIFTEEN
OUR FAMILY

I turned forty-six a couple of weeks before I became a bishop. I was far removed from Fogo, both in my professional and private life. Both have been blessings to me. My family has always been a joy. Selma grew up in St. Anthony, the daughter of Clement and Myra (Stone) Penney, a sister to Thomas, Roy, and Paul. Selma spent three years in education at Memorial University and a year at the University of Toronto, graduating from Memorial with a Bachelor of Arts degree in education in 1957.

Selma attended her graduation dance with Edmund Moulton, also a 1957 graduate in education. I took Elizabeth Hicks, later Elizabeth Walters, to her 1957 graduation dance. In the course of the mingling and mixing that evening I met Selma Carlson Penney and we had at least one dance together.

Following graduation, Selma's teaching career took her to Port Union, St. Anthony, North West River, and Curtis Academy in St. John's.

While on a trip to St. John's from Happy Valley in 1961, and visiting Sterling and Mabel Cobb, both from Fogo Island, Selma and I met again. Whether or not it was intentional on their part, we will never know, but Selma and I arrived at the Cobbs' home, 18 Carson Avenue in St. John's, at the same time. Sterling and Mabel had a plan for the evening, which took the four of us on a car ride. Selma felt motion sickness coming on, called Sterling to stop, while she got out quickly rather than mess up the inside of the car. She was embarrassed, but it didn't dampen our attraction for one another.

Stewart and Selma, wedding day, October 11, 1962

Stewart and Selma's wedding, October 11, 1962, at All Saints Church, Foxtrap. Left to right: David Lawton, Rev. Frank Reid, Stewart, Selma, Elva Fizzard, Ruby Baikie.

Left: Selma's mother, Myra Penney
Right: Selma's father, Clement Penney

Left: Selma, teacher at Curtis Academy in St. John's
Right: Selma Carson Penney at her graduation from MUN in 1957

In 1961, she was a grade two teacher at Curtis Academy in St. John's. For the next year we saw very little of each other but corresponded regularly by letter. During her 1961 Christmas holidays, with my encouragement Selma was able to pay a visit to some of her friends in Happy Valley—Ruby and Harry Baikie and Clarence and Bella Brown, old friends from North West River days. Considering the possibility of marriage, we both gave it a lot of thought. Many of the decisions we make in life affect only ourselves, but marriage is very different. It means a decision for life that affects another special person, both families, friends, and the wider community.

Selma's family home in St. Anthony

We married October 11, 1962, at All Saints Church in Foxtrap, Conception Bay, with Bishop J. A. Meaden officiating. We chose Foxtrap rather than St. Anthony or Fogo because we both wanted a quiet wedding, no big reception, no fuss or bother. In the meantime, Selma's cousin Lilly Burry (Bill), who lived on Grenfell Avenue in St. John's, and with whom Selma boarded while teaching in St. John's, gave us the opportunity of a reception by inviting the wedding party and a few friends back to her home on Grenfell Avenue after the marriage service in Foxtrap. The wedding party, beside ourselves, consisted of Elva (Blake) Fizzard and Ruby (Burt) Baikie on Selma's side, and David Lawton and Frank Reid on my side, and Selma's uncle, Reverend Dr. Lester Burry, the father-giver. Following the reception, we flew off to Montreal for our honeymoon. From Montreal we flew back to establish our first home together in Happy Valley.

For the delivery of our first child, Selma went back home to St. Anthony. I joined Selma a week before Carla Ann was born, August 6, 1963. We flew back on the Grenfell Mission plane from St. Anthony to Goose Bay with a stop in North West River. We got off the plane in North West River while preparations were being made for the last leg of the trip. As I walked up the wharf in my clerical attire, proudly holding our baby in my arms, I met Dr. Anthony Paddon. He stopped as if to size up the situation, and with a broad smile he said, "Reverend Payne, you look very domesticated."

Our second child, Christopher Stewart, was born September 6, 1964, at the Grenfell Mission nursing station in Happy Valley. It was in the wee hours of Sunday morning that he arrived, and I shared the good news with the worshiping congregation some hours afterwards.

Veronica, daughter of Moses and Susie Dyson, was one of a very large family in Happy Valley. Relationships in the family had come to an all-time low because of the excessive use of alcohol, which led to physical abuse and neglect. The father would beat the mother, even during a pregnancy, sometimes in front of the children, which naturally caused them to be afraid and very unhappy. Veronica had quit school in grade eight and had run away from home. She was staying with relatives and acquaintances, whoever would take her in. We had her babysit our children on a few occasions, and we had much empathy for her.

Selma and I knew Veronica's situation well. We talked about it again and again and felt that we should do something to help her. Could we take her to live with us? How would she fit in? How would she make out? How would we make out, suddenly having a teenager in the family? How would Carla and Chris adapt to having a much older sibling? We gave it much careful thought and decided to offer Veronica a home with our family. Nearing the time when we would move to Bay Roberts, we approached Veronica and her parents about the possibility of her becoming a part of our family. The parents had no problem with that and Veronica was quite excited about the prospect. She was fourteen at the time, so we didn't go through formal adoption procedures. She moved in with us, thereafter as our chosen daughter. We all adapted and did extremely well.

We moved from Happy Valley to Bay Roberts in 1965 with the three children, Carla, Chris, and Veronica. Carla and Chris were too young to be much affected by the move. They both started school at the amalgamated school in Bay Roberts. For Veronica, it was an exciting time as she got back to school and made new friends. She completed grades nine, ten, and eleven in Bay Roberts and went to nurses training at the Grace Hospital in St. John's.

While in Bay Roberts, Selma and I thought it would be a good idea to get a dog as a pet for the children. We checked out the different pedigrees and finally settled on a Brittany spaniel named Sandy. Sandy was a very good pet, but I had never taken her for proper training and didn't have time to train her myself. On walks, she would pull frantically, turning a walk into a run. The lower pane of glass in the outside door to our back porch, for some unknown reason, was missing for a while. When the inside door was open, Sandy would bound through the opening and into the porch. This particular day, I replaced the glass in the outside door, and soon afterwards I went up through the garden to untie Sandy. Sandy was so excited and full of energy she made a beeline for the house. As I watched, I knew exactly what was going to happen. She went straight through the pane of glass and into the porch. Except for the scare, there was no injury. The laugh was on me, having to fix the door all over again and try to teach Sandy to respect my efforts.

Our third child, our son Robert Clement, was born in the Grace Hospital in St. John's on January 7, 1967. On the way into St. John's to bring mother and baby home, my gas gauge was registering low and I knew I had to get gas before leaving St. John's. I hastened onto the Trans-Canada Highway (TCH) with mother and baby on board. However, in the excitement of the moment I forgot all about the gas. By the time I realized it, I knew that I didn't have enough gas to get anywhere near Bay Roberts. It was a frosty January day. The only solution was to leave the TCH and see if we could make it to Holyrood for gas. We made it safely to Holyrood, bought some gas and, much relieved, made our way to Bay Roberts on the old Conception Bay Highway.

I had hoped to have a year of theological study in England. In fact, Bishop Meaden had promised me that, but taking on a new parish, the Parish of Bay Roberts, the chances of doing so in the foreseeable future were very slim. In the spring of 1967 I availed of the opportunity to take a three-week tour of England and Scotland, with a couple of days in Lisbon, Portugal. Selma had had a similar tour with some friends following her graduation, and knowing how I had looked forward to visiting England, she encouraged me to go on the tour. I flew to London, England, where I joined the tour group. The tour took in a great many cities and towns from London to Edinburgh, including stops at a number of cathedrals and castles. It was all so interesting and educational, but it was difficult being away from the family and thinking of Selma at home with the four children, and Robert only six months old. It was the chance of a lifetime to visit in and around Lisbon, Portugal, but being alone so far away from home and not being able to speak the language made me feel pretty homesick at times. Wherever I have travelled over the years, it was always so good to get back home, and especially so following this trip.

While we lived in Bay Roberts, with St. John's little more than an hour away, for a period of time I took Carla to ballet lessons every Saturday morning. Carla quite enjoyed the excursion and the ballet, but after a while she went on to other things at home.

The door to my study in Bay Roberts had several panes of glass in it. One day, when all my reasoning with Robert to leave me alone to do some work in my study failed, I went into the study and closed the door. Robert made a run for the door and drove his right arm through a pane of glass. He gave himself some nasty cuts and scratches and kept me to his side for a while. The same little boy, one day when our attention was turned to Veronica and her readiness for the Grace Hospital in St. John's, somehow got access to a bottle of baby aspirin and was quiet for the longest time. When our attention turned to him, it was obvious that he had eaten some of the aspirin, but we couldn't tell how many. We immediately went to the Janeway Children's Hospital in St. John's, where they checked him out and found nothing of great concern.

Our four children: Carla, Christopher, Robert, and Angela

To complete our family, Angela Marie Louise arrived October 26, 1970, shortly after our move from Bay Roberts to St. Anthony. She was born in Charles Curtis Memorial Hospital in St. Anthony, and for the first time I accompanied Selma into the case room and witnessed the birth, a miracle to be sure. Every birth is a miracle in that it is beyond our comprehension, understanding, and control.

The move from Bay Roberts to St. Anthony was one of the easier ones for our children, because they were more familiar with St. Anthony and had Pop Penney and other relatives there. Carla and Chris entered school in the integrated system in St. Anthony in September 1970, Robert was off to school in September 1972, and Angela joined them in September 1975.

In busy parish life, it is a balancing act to give to one's family and the parish the time and attention they both need and deserve. Emergencies occur without being scheduled, and at the call I would be off to the side of the person or persons affected. Also, the only time working people can be available for meetings is at night. Night after night there would be a meeting somewhere in the parish, sometimes more than one meeting a night. The people who were short-changed on my time were my family. My consolation was that Selma was always there with the children when I had to be out and about the parish at night meetings. Later on, as bishop, my travels in the diocese and outside took me away a lot, but the children were older then and less dependent on me.

I always made a practice of getting away together with the family on our summer holidays. Selma's brother Paul and his wife, Rebecca, lived in Debert, Nova Scotia. Several summers when holiday time rolled around, we packed up and went to Nova Scotia. Using Paul's canvas-top trailer, we spent the time in some of the parks in Nova Scotia and Prince Edward Island. I later purchased a canvas-top trailer from Selma's brother Tom.

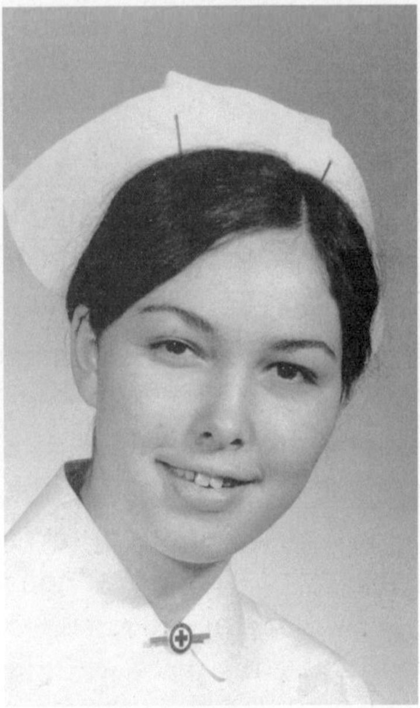

Veronica, who became part of our family in 1965 at age fourteen, now a licensed practical nurse.

The summer of 1972, the Reverend Cyrus Pitman, while still rector of Flower's Cove parish—later bishop of Eastern Newfoundland and Labrador—and I decided to do the six-week supervised pastoral education course at the Nova Scotia Sanitarium in Kentville, Nova Scotia, from late June to early August. Our supervisor was the Rev. Dr. Howard H. Taylor.

Cyrus and I each rented a house trailer for our families in New Minas and worked from there.

That summer I towed our canvas-top trailer all the way from St. Anthony to Nova Scotia and back again. The Northern Peninsula Highway was not yet paved. Before we left Nova Scotia to come home that summer I purchased a large sheet of foam, thinking that it would serve well on top of the mattress. I placed it underneath the top covering of the trailer and proceeded homeward. When we arrived home in St. Anthony and opened up the camper, the sheet of foam was a dark brown colour, full of dust from the unpaved road. I didn't want to throw it away. Could it be washed out? I wondered. The only way to find out was to try it. Upstairs I went with the sheet of foam and immersed it in warm water in the bathtub. The more I worked on it the more water it absorbed and the heavier it got, while still retaining the dark brown colour. I wrung it out as best I could and placed it on the outdoor clothesline to dry. After several warm, sunny days it did dry out but never got the use for which it was intended.

One afternoon in February 1973, as chairman of the school board, I was about to go to the school board office to sign the bus contracts for the year. Before doing so I went to the bathroom with Dr. Kubler Ross's new book, *Death and Dying*, in hand. As I sat there reading the book, I heard the crackling sound of wood burning. I thought, *If that is fire, the house is gone.* As I came from the bathroom in a hurry, I saw fire dropping from a light fixture in one bedroom and smoke escaping from several corners.

Selma was a substitute teacher in the school where Chris and Carla were students. I immediately rushed Angela and the babysitter, Selma Patey, over next door to Alfred Anderson's house. In the meantime, I saw Robert and his friend playing on the lower road. While next door I telephoned the fire department, then ran back to the parsonage. I opened the porch door but couldn't enter because the place was full of smoke. The firemen came instantly, and when the fire was out, men from all around entered the house to salvage what they could of our possessions. Within a couple of hours, all that we owned was lying on the side of the road in banks of snow. From there it was carried to St. Mary's Church basement.

Late that afternoon a snowstorm blew in, and traffic was halted to the point that Selma and I decided to walk around the harbour to her father's place. On the way we stopped in at St. Mary's Church basement. It was a sobering experience to see the salvaged contents of our home scattered all over the basement floor. It made us think, more than ever before, about the insignificance of material things.

That night, at Pop Penney's and Uncle Roy's place, we held one another closer than ever before, realizing how fortunate we were that the fire broke out in the afternoon and not in the middle of the night. To this day we are very grateful that only material things were lost. We are grateful also for the kind and generous help that we received from parishioners, former parishioners, and friends. The Grenfell Mission provided us with one of their houses, the bungalow, for the remainder of the year until the new parsonage was ready for occupancy.

The move from St. Anthony to Corner Brook in 1978 was the more difficult move for the children. They had spent more years in St. Anthony than anywhere else and were leaving behind not only friends but close relatives, especially Pop Penny. They were anxious to get back to St. Anthony in the summer of 1979 for all too short a stay. When we were about to leave for Corner Brook, Robert was unaccounted for. When I found him it was clear that he didn't want to leave St. Anthony. I had to pick him up and put him in the car, kicking and screaming.

I'm not aware that our children suffered any from being "the preacher's kids." Selma and I always let them know that they were the same as other children, no more, no less, and should not be treated differently from others. Along the way they were involved in the usual children and youth activities through school, church, and community programs. We never wanted to choose their professions or life's work for them. All we asked was that they be good people wherever they went and at whatever they did.

Carla, Chris, Robert, and Angela accompanied Selma and me to England as I attended Lambeth Conference 1978 at the University of Kent in Canterbury, England. As bishops' families had to live off campus, we were fortunate at a late date to find a place for Selma and the children at Dover Castle, with the keeper of the castle, Col. Maurice Atherton and his wife, Wendi, and their children, Jamie and Christine. The children had a fabulous time staying at the castle and seeing much of the places and events around Dover. I got out to the castle with them in my free time. They came to Canterbury when things were happening to which families were invited. The Athertons are marvellous people and were so kind to Selma, the children, and me. Thirty-six years later we still keep in touch, at least with a Christmas greeting each year.

On completing high school, all five of our children went on to further education. Veronica, through her studies at the Grace Hospital in St. John's, became a licensed practical nurse and worked at the hospital in St. Anthony until her official retirement in 2011. She still goes in to work part-time. Veronica and her husband, Scott Cull, raised three children: Kenny, Robert, and Kathy.

Carla went to Memorial University in St. John's and studied early childhood development. She works in the Fisher daycare centre at the College of the North Atlantic (CNA) in Corner Brook. Carla and her husband, Nelson Adams (now ex-husband), built their home in Little Rapids. They have five children: Ben and Stefany (Carla's stepchildren), and Liam, Jake, and Elyse.

Chris, all the way through, was interested in food preparation and services. He trained as a chef at the Bay St. George community college, now College of the North Atlantic, in Stephenville. He and his wife, Lana (Goodyear), made their home in Massey Drive, near Corner Brook. They have two sons, Scott and Matthew. Chris works as a chef in Cambridge Bay, two months on and a month off.

Robert attended Memorial University, St. John's campus, in the Faculty of Engineering and graduated as a civil engineer. He and his wife, Denise (Aucoin), made their home in Corner Brook. They have two children, Alexandra and Andrew. Robert is in the business of construction with Marine Contractors.

Angela entered the Faculty of Education at Memorial University, St. John's campus, and graduated as a licensed teacher. For the first five years after graduating, she taught school in Iqaluit, Nunavut. Angela and her husband, Kenny Ford, made their home in Corner Brook, where they both work. They have three children: Dylan (Angela's stepson), and Steven and Laura.

It was some time after I retired that Selma and I decided to respond to at least one of the many requests to help educate a young person in Africa. For two years we financially supported Edith Nakalanzi through her training to be a nurse at Kavull School of Nursing and Midwifery in Kampala, Uganda. We did it through the School of Nursing and didn't have a lot of contact with Edith herself, though she did write to thank us a couple of times. We haven't heard from her for some time now.

Selma did not plan to teach after we were married but got called on to substitute for extended periods of time in Happy Valley, Bay Roberts, St. Anthony, and Corner Brook. One former student, Anna Marie (Adams) Cartwright, whom we hear from every Christmas, once wrote this on a Christmas card. I quote a part of what she said: "Dear Mrs. Payne. Just a little card to say thank you for the positive impact you made in my life both in the Valley and how even now your strength, presence and understanding continue to be part of my daily journey. Your acceptance gave me courage and belief in myself. My life has been guided by your caring example and sincerity. Today I work as an educator in a local daycare. I now understand that a simple kind word or a glance can't help but be life-changing."

Selma has been my greatest gift in life, naturally quiet and unassuming, a tower of strength to me throughout the years. She has been a model wife, mother, grandmother, and friend. Though she had every right, she never, ever played her hand as the rector's wife when I was in parish ministry, or as the bishop's wife when I was in diocesan office. She always had her own ministry, exercised her God-given gifts like other women in the parish and in the diocese, always through women's organizations such as the Anglican Church Women and through church and community choirs. She resisted, for the most part, taking an office in any organization but made her contribution shoulder to shoulder with all the other members.

Left to right: Angela, Selma, Stewart, Robert, Carla, and Chris in behind

Selma and Stewart with Veronica in Little Rapids

Selma never complained about my having to be away from home a lot, especially during the nearly twenty years of my active episcopate. She understood what was expected of me and supported me fully. She would never telephone me at the office or allow the children to telephone. If on the very rare occasion my secretary said, "That's your wife on the telephone," I knew it was an urgent matter that could not wait until I got home. Again and again the children would be told, "Wait until Dad comes home." Sometimes that could be a warning because one or the other had misbehaved. By the time Dad came home it was all forgotten.

Selma loved people, children particularly, and always had time for everyone. She was always sympathetic and positive in her opinions about people and never spoke ill of anyone. She seemed to go by the standard, "If you can't say something good about a person, don't say anything." Hospitality was her forte. She sometimes dreamed about having a little tea room and catering to friends at afternoon teas. Oftentimes I brought a person home with me at a mealtime, even when I wasn't in a position to warn Selma. I would issue the invitation for a cup of tea, knowing that a cup of tea was always available. For Selma it had to be more than a cup of tea. I can hear her now saying, "At mealtime you can't offer just a cup of tea. It has to be more than that." In an instant, there would be a full-course meal.

I surprise myself in my restraint in not recounting Selma's and my blessings of being grandparents. That story, too, would be a joy to relate, but let me get on with more about being bishop.

CHAPTER SIXTEEN
WESTERN NEWFOUNDLAND, 1978–1997

Very soon after my ordination as bishop I was off to the 1978 Lambeth Conference in Canterbury, England. It is difficult to put into words the feeling of being one of 400 bishops walking in procession up through Canterbury Cathedral, singing, "At the name of Jesus, every knee shall bow, every tongue confess him, King of glory now," and to be warmly welcomed by Archbishop Coggan of Canterbury. That was the first of many exposures to people whose language, race, and culture broadened the outlook of a fellow from Fogo. Those blessings must await my recounting some of the blessings I encountered at home. I will not attempt to encompass twenty years but rather share with you stories that may give a sense of my ministry as a bishop.

On returning from Lambeth in 1978, I was eager to get started with my ministry as diocesan bishop. The diocesan synod office was in the Millbrook Mall and had one small main office with one corner partitioned off as a small office for the bishop. The secretary treasurer, Mrs. Jean Clarke, occupied the remaining space. Lining one wall in the office were a few books, mainly Bibles, and prayer- and hymn books on consignment from the Anglican Book Centre in Toronto, as a service to people in our diocese.

With the help of Jean Clarke, my secretary, and my episcopal commissary, Reverend Charles Abraham—my representative in my absence—I was brought up-to-date on what was happening while I attended the Lambeth Conference. Having been a parish priest for the past twenty-one years and involved to some extent in diocesan affairs, I believed I had a fair understanding of the work before me. It didn't take long to become familiar with and to find my place in the diocesan, provincial, and national church structures.

Time had to be spent in the diocesan office, but my priority was to be out and about the diocese with the people. Every visit was special. It was a joy to be hosted by the family in the rectories and in other homes in the parishes. People who didn't know the bishop personally or hadn't had a previous visit could be a little bit apprehensive at the thought of his coming for a meal.

On one of my visits to the Parish of Grand Bay, the rector, the Reverend Martin Lane, asked Gordon Matthews if he and Phyllis might have me for Sunday dinner. Gordon and Phyllis had two small boys, Stephen and Paul. When Gordon informed Phyllis that I was coming to dinner, she was troubled and said, "What we have is not good enough for the bishop. The boys' toys will be all over the place. The house will be untidy. How will I ever manage?" The plan was carried through and Phyllis soon discovered that her fears were ill-founded. We enjoyed a great meal together and had a delightful time being entertained by the boys. Gordon and Phyllis got to see me as a real person, like themselves, with children who were once the ages of Stephen and Paul. From that day on I have had a standing invitation to their home anytime I'm in Grand Bay.

A great deal of my attention and energy was directed to personnel matters, getting the right people for the right parishes, and being a pastor to the pastors. I felt I should always be available to them, not only in parish visits, but to have an open-door policy to my office in the diocesan synod office, an annual clergy retreat, and an annual clergy conference.

As chief pastor of the diocese I could do only a small portion of the pastoral care myself. I expected the clergy to be diligent in their pastoral duties to all their parishioners, especially the elderly, sick, and shut in, and at times when preparation is being done for holy baptism, marriages, and burials. Preparation is important, but more important still is follow-up and pastoral care after the event.

Whenever I visited a parish in the diocese, as much as time would allow, I would, with the rector, visit the elderly, sick, and shut-in folk in their homes or in hospital. A particular visit stands out in my mind. In the Parish of Rose Blanche, the Reverend Glenn Small and I set out to do some visiting. In one upstairs bedroom we sat beside the bed of an elderly bedridden lady and shared some thoughts and prayers. When we were leaving she said, "I get ready for bed at night, as the lights in the nearby houses disappear. I say my prayers and I remember you in my prayers every night." I couldn't find words to adequately thank her, I was so deeply moved. I think she knew that I was very grateful. On any given night I could be in my car travelling home to Corner Brook from any corner of the far-flung diocese, after a busy parish visit, and knowing that she and others were praying for me was a blessed gift. Pastoral care is the key to the church's life and future, and it is carried on by lay people as well as ordained folk, all representing Christ and His Church.

While in the Parish of Rose Blanche another time, the Reverend Glenn Small and I were again visiting parishioners. As we approached a certain house, instead of keeping to the path leading to the house, I tried to show how agile I was by running up over a slanting boulder. In the process of that escapade, my face came into contact with a clothesline. There was little damage except to my pride, and the loss of my eyeglasses. Sometime afterwards, one cold, windy March day, while on my way to a clergy gathering, at the Doon Lodge in the Stephenville area, I ran out of gas on Gallant's Hill. This necessitated a long delay as I had to hitchhike back to a gas station, without a gas can. The attendant at the station very graciously found a gas can, filled it up, and gave me a ride back to my car. When I finally arrived at Doon Lodge, I embarrassingly had to tell why I was delayed. At the end of the clergy gathering, while taking leave of one another, the Reverend Glenn Small called attention to all present and, on behalf of the clergy, presented me with a rope clothesline and a five-gallon gas tank. I think I gave the clothesline to someone who needed a piece of rope one day, but I still have the gas tank.

To assure equal time and attention to each parish, I sent out to parish clergy a yearly schedule of parish visits for confirmations and pastoral care. All parishes, in time, received additional visits around the clergy appointment process, the consecration of parish property, an ordination, a special anniversary, or a synod. In a few instances, visits were necessary to deal with a troubling issue. In the back of this book I have listed one year's schedule, typical of most. APPENDIX A.

When my schedule would take me to a parish for confirmation on a Sunday, I normally went out to that parish on the Saturday and stayed overnight with the family at the rectory. On one rare occasion, that weekend when the clocks sprang ahead one hour, having arrived home late Saturday from a week of meetings abroad, I informed the Parish of Cow Head that I would come to them in good time for the eleven o'clock Sunday morning service. Early that Sunday morning I was off to the Parish of Cow Head, where the Reverend Stewart Bellows was then the rector. At about ten thirty, as I approached St. Mary's Church in Cow Head, the road in front of the church was lined off with cars, and people were going inside. Assuming that Stewart would be in the church by now, instead of going farther on to the rectory I parked my car and went into the church. Stewart hadn't yet arrived. I proceeded to robe and prepare for the confirmation service, expecting Stewart momentarily. At five minutes to eleven, the realization that he may not have advanced his clock was beginning to settle in, so I sent one of the men to check on him. A few minutes after eleven o'clock, the embarrassed-looking rector hastened into the packed church, full of apologies for forgetting to advance his clock one hour. Apart from being a bit late starting, the service went well. Stewart has never been allowed to forget that incident.

In Ramea, an island on the South Coast of Newfoundland, the Anglican Church Women had made a new, fair linen cloth for the altar in St. Boniface Church. The rector, the Reverend George Spencer, asked the women if he could use the cloth right away. The women were afraid that the cloth might get soiled, so they decided to keep it and first use it when the bishop came on his next parish visit. I made the visit to Ramea and saw—and appreciated—the beautiful cloth now in use for the first time. I presided at the confirmation of a large number of young people and at the Holy Eucharist. In the midst of the service, while preparing the altar I accidentally spilled wine all over the centre of the cloth. I was devastated, but the rector was not at all alarmed, and he was able to tease the ladies about that for a long time afterwards.

In June of 1979, the International Grenfell Association invited me to be one of the speakers at a conference at the Charles Curtis Memorial hospital in St. Anthony. My subject was "Pastoral care to the elderly." I went to St. Anthony the day before the conference and in the evening called on a number of people, including Roy and June Andrews, who lived across the road from the Anglican rectory. Roy had been the parish treasurer for several years during my time in the parish. Roy and June were our very good friends. Roy informed me that he and June had acquired a mobile camper and had planned to go camping that weekend, but because I was going to be in St. Anthony they decided to stay home. He also talked about how he had taken up scuba diving. I expressed some concern about the dangers inherent in scuba diving without training and expert advice. Roy assured me that he was aware of the dangers and had acquired a degree of confidence in the art of scuba diving.

The next day, as the conference was in process, I was called out to take an emergency telephone call. The rector of St. Anthony parish, the Reverend Bill Watts, informed me that Roy Andrews had drowned while scuba diving with a friend in the Big Brook area. I couldn't believe what I was hearing. I was devastated. This might not have happened if he had followed his plan to go camping on the weekend instead of staying home on my behalf. Who's to tell? My visit to St. Anthony was much prolonged as I spent considerable time with the distraught families and friends and took part in Roy's funeral service. The sudden loss of my very good friend leaves a deep hurt to this day. While writing this I telephoned June, now living in Baie Verte, and we talked about what happened in 1979 and got caught up on the news about our families and friends. The day I telephoned June was the thirty-fourth anniversary of Roy's death.

It was a waning tradition, a carry-over from the days when the bishop could only visit briefly every four or five years, to build a bell arch of fir boughs at the church entrance, with a sign in bold letters atop proclaiming "WELCOME TO OUR BISHOP." It was not uncommon, years ago, for some congregations to decorate their churches, and at the arrival of the bishop's boat to fire off powder guns. With the much more frequent visits from the bishop, those traditions have given way to other signs of welcome. However, I had the experience of walking underneath an arch in many of my parish visits and thanking the folks for taking all that care.

On my way driving up the Northern Peninsula one day, I stopped in Portland Creek to see Elizabeth Payne, affectionately known as Aunt Cookie, who was bedridden. She had no idea that I was near the place until her caregiver directed me to her bedside. Her first remark was, "What, the bishop is here and there is neither arch up?"

My response was, "Aunt Cookie, if they built an arch every time I came by, the forest would be bare." We had a very good visit without an arch of boughs.

Being on a number of national church committees and a member of the national House of Bishops meant a fair bit of travel to and from Toronto, mainly from Deer Lake Airport. I travelled easily, always had a book in hand, and wrote many letters and notes as I travelled. I did occasionally doze off, too. In anticipation of a meeting in Toronto, on one occasion the Reverend Kirby Walsh, the hospital chaplain in Corner Brook, offered to give me a ride to Deer Lake Airport. As we entered the terminal with luggage in hand, the place was unusually quiet. I went up to the Air Canada ticket counter and produced my ticket to the attendant, only to be told that that particular flight was not out of Deer Lake but Stephenville. I was so used to flying out of Deer Lake and hadn't checked my ticket carefully enough to realize the change in place of departure. I was more than a little embarrassed. Kirby took me home again, but later that evening I did get a flight out of Deer Lake and arrived a little late for my meetings.

Another time, en route to Toronto on an Air Canada flight, there was a slight smell of smoke, and the pilot announced that he was making an unscheduled landing in Montreal. We were advised to leave all personal belongings on board and disembark promptly via the emergency chutes. Buses met us as we disembarked and took us into the terminal. After two or three hours we were allowed to board the plane again. As we were walking toward the plane a lady passenger came up to me and said, "I'm some glad you were on that plane with us today." There are things about the clerical collar that attract some people, and, conversely, keep others at a distance.

In 1978, the Diocese of Western Newfoundland was made up of nineteen parishes. The rural parishes were very large, geographically and numerically. Flower's Cove parish, for example, which stretched from Eddies Cove West to Eddies Cove East, was comprised of seventeen congregations. Some were quite small but needed, no less, the same schedule of worship services and pastoral care. We had reached the stage in Flower's Cove parish when an assistant priest was stationed in Plum Point. The Parish of St. Anthony, all the while I was rector, 1970 to 1978, had ten congregations. In large, somewhat isolated parishes, clergy could easily become frustrated and disheartened, resulting in short tenures.

A good supply of well-equipped clergy in smaller, more manageable areas, and more lay involvement, was part of my vision for the diocese. The national church program "Anglicans In Mission (AIM)," a program of spiritual renewal and financial development, was just coming on stream and would afford us the opportunity to do some reorganization of the larger parishes. In the financial development part of the program, the whole Canadian Church together would endeavour to raise $40 million. Twenty million would be returned to the dioceses for local initiatives. Nine million would be allocated to fund mission needs and opportunities in northern Canada. Six million would be provided for work overseas, and $5 million would be allocated to strengthen the pensions of clergy and lay professionals, who had retired many years earlier and were receiving very small pensions. Each of the thirty dioceses across Canada was assessed a fair share of the total amount ($40 million) to be raised. Our diocesan share in Western Newfoundland was $1,060,000.

The organization and planning of the AIM program began in the summer of 1981, having been overwhelmingly approved by the National Executive Council of General Synod in May. The question in all our hearts and minds was, "What is God calling us to be and to do at this time?" The mission's study phase began in January 1982 and would continue throughout the program. The financial development, giving each Anglican an opportunity to make a financial commitment in support of mission and ministry over a five-year period, began early in 1983.

Structures were put in place, the appropriate committees were struck, and we were off and running with direction, help, and support from professional fundraisers, whom the national church had hired.

Before anything else could happen, the bishop in each of the thirty dioceses across Canada had to get commitments for several major gifts. A major gift commitment could be any amount from $2000 and up per year for five years. I was not accustomed to inviting people to make such commitments and had my very difficult moments. However, it had to be done. Eventually I made the appointments to visit some people, shared the story of AIM, and gave people the opportunity to consider what they wanted to do. The results were astonishing. Every person contacted realized that it wasn't just about money. Each visit was a pastoral visit concerning our Christian stewardship. No one was made to feel that they had to do anything. After hearing about AIM, we reflected together on where we were with the church and what we felt God might be calling us to be and do at this time. Whether the answer was yes or not at this time, or plain no, the visits were great and very fruitful. If a parishioner couldn't make a commitment of money, that was understandable, but the subject of ministry and mission, involving all members of the Body of Christ, the Church, was opened up. We saw a number of people get back to regular weekly worship as a result. At one Saturday evening visit, for example, one couple made a commitment of money, but what was more important, they were both in church the next morning after being absent for years.

I will not give the names of people who gave those first gifts because everyone's gift, big or small, according to means, is equally as important. The smaller gift from one person could represent more of a sacrifice than the larger gift from someone else. We gave up publishing names, and amounts given, years ago.

In the visit that resulted in my first major gift, I explained the

AIM program, and the place of major gifts in it, and said to the person that he might want to take time to consider it. His response was, "I'll commit $5,000 a year for five years." I nearly fell off my chair! He sensed how I was feeling and quietly added with a smile, "That's all right, Bishop, its only money, after all." He became much more involved in the life of the church in the diocese and remarked often how it had saved his life. He had retired just before the AIM program came to be and, being alone, felt isolated with no purpose in life. AIM and related activities gave him purpose and meaning and something to do and to be.

On another occasion, after explaining the program and the place of a major gift to an elderly retired couple, the husband replied, "Yes, we would like to give on that level."

His wife said, "What level, dear? The bishop said from $2,000 up."

He replied, "$5,000 a year for five years."

She said, "That's all right. You know what we can afford."

I could hardly believe my ears and kept offering more time for them to think about their commitment. I could come back later. The husband got up and left the room. In a few minutes he returned and placed $5,000 in cash on the table in front of me and said, "I can't give you a cheque for it at this time, but here is the cash if you don't mind taking cash." I was amazed and almost speechless. But what he said after that was what mattered most: "I knew we were not giving to the church as we ought and could, and I've been meaning to talk to the rector about that. We didn't know anything about AIM. You have come and told us about it, and it was as if that money were put away for that purpose."

I thought, *If there are people out there who have money put away for AIM, then I had better keep going.* One could only be grateful, inspired, and encouraged by responses like that. In the second year of AIM, that man turned up at the synod office with his second-year commitment of $5,000, in cash, and thereafter remitted his yearly amount to National Office, as was the plan, and National Office would later send us our diocesan share.

The Parish of Pasadena–Cormack was at the same time fundraising to replace St. David's Church in Pasadena, which had been destroyed by fire. It must have seemed impossible to run the AIM program at the same time, and one evening a parishioner telephoned me to say, "Can we be excused from involvement in the AIM program?"

My answer, as sympathetic as I was toward their situation, was, "We have to press on and give the people in every parish the opportunity to know about AIM and to decide for themselves. We can't make decisions for them." Later that night I received another telephone call thanking me for my stand and informing me that one person who was visited that night had committed to a gift of money and two acres of land on which to build the new St. David's Church. It so excited me that I couldn't fall asleep for the longest time that night.

As we proceeded with the AIM program, many people got involved in stewardship study and as regular visitors. The majority of our people in Western Newfoundland were contacted, with marvellous results. Some could not commit to a monetary gift. We understood that, and in a few cases we directed people to where they could get help for themselves, but without exception they appreciated being thought about and contacted. It made people feel important and to realize, as well, that money is only one symbol of the gifts that God has given us. We have many, many more gifts that we use in God's service to the world. The AIM program was successful in Western Newfoundland, not only in the financial development aspect, but in our reaching out to one another and sharing the opportunity to be informed and to be more active in mission and ministry. Christian stewardship is indeed about much more than money, but money is a part of it and there are times, in the life of the church, when we have to call it like it is.

The process of reorganizing the diocese into smaller parishes was studied by parishes themselves, synod office staff, and the synod executive committee approved and implemented the changes. The number of parishes grew from nineteen to thirty-two as the diocese was able, through the resources of AIM, to make grants to enable the building of new rectories and help employ another priest. Reorganizing in some of the larger parishes was a bit overdue, and those parishes moved fairly quickly through the process. In other parishes, where the numbers of people and the resources were less but the geography was unmanageable, we proceeded at a slower pace but gave it considerable thought, to give it a chance. Reorganizing is always a work in progress.

At a special service in the Pro Cathedral on January 13, 1985, I had the privilege and honour of designating St. John the Evangelist Church as the Cathedral Church of the Diocese of Western Newfoundland. At the same service three canons were installed: the Reverend Thomas Moulton, diocesan stewardship officer and program coordinator; the Reverend Leonard Whitten, rector of the Parish of Port aux Basques; and the Reverend John Brown, rector of the Parish of Seal Cove. Leonard and John were prevented from attending because of bad weather. Mr. Allan Seaborn had succeeded Mr. Clyde Wells as our chancellor. He was present and took part in the special service.

To further the work of reorganizing, the diocese took on another financial development program, encouraged by the national church office, called "Faith In Action (FIA)." This was a far less ambitious program than AIM, but the members of each parish, on the basis of income and numbers of people, were asked to raise their fair share for work in the diocese and in their own parish. The work proceeded rather smoothly, but a few parishes lagged behind.

While FIA was in progress, I made a pastoral visit to an elderly lady in one of our parishes after the Sunday morning worship service. In the course of the visit she indicated that she had an important matter she wanted dealt with and that I might be the person to talk to about it. Now was not the time, so I went back, at her request, some days later. The matter was this: she had some money she wanted to share with the church in her parish and diocese. I was amazed and explained that I saw this fitting right into the FIA program her parish and diocese were engaged in. She agreed wholeheartedly and proceeded to ask her daughter-in-law to get the money and count it out. It came to a staggering total of $23,000. I was dumfounded, extremely humbled, and more than grateful. This amount was a large part of that parish's FIA fair share. They were on the road to great success before they had actually started.

Archdeacon Gerald Colbourne and I made many visits to parishes, encouraging them all to get on board with the FIA program. On one particular visit, before our presentations began we were informed that the parish council had decided not to get involved in FIA. My response was standard. It wasn't up to the parish council to decide; the diocesan synod, with representatives from every parish present, had made the decision, and we should get the information out to our people and let them decide what they can do. We continued with our FIA story, and at the end of the meeting the parish council was all for it. One person remarked to the archdeacon afterwards, "The bishop could sell ice cubes to people in the frozen north."

A later visit to another parish one night didn't produce the same results. We weren't making much progress. As we drove away from there that night, the archdeacon, with a tired smirk on his face, said to me, "You didn't sell any ice cubes tonight, Bishop." I had to agree.

Overall, though, the FIA program did produce some resources to further our work of reorganizing in the cause of ministry and mission.

I don't know if we would have done things differently with respect to making smaller parishes if we had seen the cod moratorium coming our way in 1992. Some of the smaller, coastal parishes we had created were hit hardest by the out-migration and have found it impossible to reach and maintain self-support. Where this has happened, it was not a failure on anyone's part. If we had to give grants-in-aid to some such parishes, so be it, we had done that down through our history when we had missions that could not be self-supporting. Several dioceses in the Council of the North, for example, are aided by the national church to this day. The failure would have been in not attempting to make smaller parishes in the first place. There are always lessons to be learned from experience. I realized that we might have to pursue some different models of doing ministry in some areas in the future.

I never thought of myself as a fundraiser and still don't, but I learned some things about myself, and people generally, as we ran the financial development programs AIM and FIA. If you are able to accept "No" as well as "Yes," you can move forward. It is fear of rejection that often immobilizes us. People like to be informed, they like to be asked, and they like to be acknowledged. Knowing what the church needs the money for is essential. If they agree that it is a worthy cause, they will support according to their means. They want to know that the church is a good steward of its resources, too.

My election and installation as metropolitan of the Ecclesiastical Province of Canada, and thus archbishop of Western Newfoundland, took place in 1990. (The name metropolitan comes from the word metropolis. In church usage the metropolitan, first among bishops in the province, is the bishop elected to have some oversight and responsibilities in a large metropolitical area, called a province.) The Ecclesiastical Province of Canada (Eastern Canada) takes in the dioceses of Montreal, Quebec, Fredericton, Nova Scotia, Prince Edward Island, Western Newfoundland, Central Newfoundland, and Eastern Newfoundland and Labrador.

As metropolitan, it would be my honour and responsibility to preside at provincial synods once every three years in one of the dioceses in the Ecclesiastical Province by turn, to preside at provincial council meetings once a year, and preside at the provincial House of Bishops meetings, which always took place around Provincial Synod and Provincial Council. The metropolitan is simply first among equals and exercises some pastoral care for bishops in the province. The metropolitan is entrusted, too, with the responsibility to see that persons newly elected to be bishops in the province are the right candidates for that ministry and are duly consecrated.

In 1991, I felt strongly the need to give more attention to prayer and proceeded to attend the Anglican Fellowship of Prayer (AFP) conference in San Antonio, Texas. In the 1940s and 1950s, two ladies in the United States, Helen Shoemaker and Polly Wiley, developed a ministry of group prayer, which in 1958 became known as "The Anglican Fellowship of Prayer." The AFP is organized in Canada, the Caribbean, as well as in the United States. AFP Canada exists to encourage and enable the ministry of prayer in Canada. It seeks to be a teaching resource to assist individuals and congregations to grow in the life of prayer.

At the San Antonio AFP conference, the prominent guest speaker was the Reverend John Claypool, an Episcopal priest in the United States, who gave several inspiring talks on prayer. There were several workshops on different aspects of prayer and we could choose to attend whatever workshops were of interest. It was all very worthwhile, encouraging, and helpful. At that conference I was introduced to the Bethel Bible Study series and was later able to bring it into two parishes in the diocese: Stephenville and Deer Lake.

When the conference was over, several of us headed for the airport by bus. When the bus stopped at the airport, the driver stood outside the bus door to offer assistance to anyone who needed it. When I stepped off the bus in front of him, he asked me to step aside and said, "Excuse me, sir, within two weeks my wife and I are expecting our first child. Would you pray for us?" He wasn't asking me to keep them in my prayers over time but to pray for them now. We stood aside and I prayed for him and his wife and the child to be born.

On entering the terminal I found my way through security and on to the gate waiting area. As I sat there reading a book on prayer, a man came up to me with the simple greeting, "I've been praying for you for years." There was no explanation as to why he should be praying for me. I knew him only slightly as a priest in the Diocese of Niagara. We renewed our acquaintance while waiting to board the plane to Canada.

My ministry as metropolitan did give me added responsibilities, but it didn't take me away from my ministry as archbishop in our own Diocese of Western Newfoundland. I would be attending provincial synods, provincial council meetings, and provincial House of Bishops meetings anyway.

During my time as metropolitan I had the privilege of being present for the installation of Andrew Hutchison as bishop of Montreal, November 4, 1990, and being the chief consecrator at the following ordinations: Bruce Stavert as bishop of Quebec, March 1991; Donald Harvey as third bishop of Eastern Newfoundland and Labrador, January 25, 1993; Frederick Hiltz as suffragan bishop of Nova Scotia and Prince Edward Island, January 18, 1995; and Leonard Whitten as coadjutor bishop of Western Newfoundland, September 29, 1997.

The Diocese of Bermuda is an extra-provincial diocese under

the oversight of the bishop of London, England. However, several of the bishops of Bermuda aligned themselves with our Ecclesiastical Province of Canada. In April of 1993, at the invitation of the bishop of Bermuda, Bishop William Down, our provincial House of Bishops meeting took place in Bermuda. The cost of travel to Bermuda was no greater than if we were meeting anywhere in eastern Canada. The church in Bermuda provided us with free accommodations. It was a great event for the bishops and their wives and much encouragement for Bishop and Mrs. Down and the church in Bermuda.

The one regret I had as metropolitan was that I was not fluent in French. Indeed, I hadn't the opportunity to study French at all. Latin was taught in most Anglican schools in my growing up. It was Latin throughout university days. Being able to speak French would have been helpful to me in my role as metropolitan, especially at gatherings in the dioceses of Quebec, Montreal, and Fredericton.

THE COD MORATORIUM

Leading up to the 1990s, because of local and foreign overfishing, cod stocks in the waters around Newfoundland were at an all-time low. The federal government declared a moratorium on the cod fishery in 1992. This put thousands of fisherfolk and fish plant workers out of work. Although the government came up with some financial assistance for displaced workers called "the package," the out-migration was great.

Soon after the moratorium was declared, I was contacted by the Roman Catholic bishop of the Diocese of Grand Falls, Newfoundland, Bishop Faber MacDonald, with the proposal of forming a coalition for fishing communities to help our unemployed fishermen and fish plant workers. Bishop MacDonald and I made contact with the churches—Anglican, Roman Catholic, United, Pentecostal, and the Salvation Army—and asked for representatives to the formative meeting. They responded well. Bishop MacDonald and I chaired that meeting and were asked to co-chair meetings of this new church coalition in the future.

Each of the churches, according to size and representation, made financial contributions like $10,000, $5,000, or $3,000 a year. It all added up to a tidy sum. In addition, we were able to get a small grant from the provincial government. The Diocese of Eastern Newfoundland and Labrador was able to give us office space in their synod office in St. John's. With the money we employed one person, Nina Patey, for a period of time. Nina was a liaison between the coalition and governments, many other organizations, and people. She put into action many of the decisions made by the coalition and looked after correspondence and the office generally. Nina's work made a great difference to the effectiveness of the coalition.

Meanwhile, there was a "Fisheries Group" in St. John's made up of Gus Etchegary, Aiden Maloney, Raymond Andrews, Mary Lou Peters, Sandy Sandemenn, Gerry Traverse, and the Reverend Ron Lee. Bishop MacDonald contacted Gus Etchegary, and as a result the Fisheries Group was able to help us with the following goals and objectives: (a) to listen to the people affected, see how they were coping, what they thought the problems were, how the church coalition could help them, and to stand by them as they had to decide on their own destiny; (b) to represent the people to governments and make sure that people received adequate compensation for their loss of employment; and (c) to do all we could to ensure that the laws of conservation were followed and the cod stocks were allowed to rebuild.

Outlining our objectives, a petition circulated by twenty-nine designated groups across the province successfully gathered 112,000 names of Newfoundlanders and Labradorians, 10,000 from Labrador. This petition was delivered to Prime Minister Jean Crétien in person in the foyer of Confederation Building in St. John's with 500 people in attendance and in front of the national press, radio and television. The prime minister gave a resounding speech and promised to present the petition to parliament.

As coalition members, we travelled fairly extensively over the island part of the province, into many of the major fishing communities in western and northern Newfoundland and the South Coast. The Fisheries Group held more meetings in the eastern part of the province. The first evening in a community, we met with the public and listened to them for their solutions to some of the problems. The next morning we met with clergy of the area and other interested people and tried to put in place a local structure to carry on the work of the coalition.

The Fisheries Group, with a small but broad range of church and community representatives, made presentations to the European Union Fishery Committee in Brussels on the state of the fishery resulting from foreign overfishing. The presentations were well-received.

Having made an intensive and effective effort in bringing the tragedy of the moratorium and the plight of our people to the attention of governments and the Canadian public, the church coalition's work was done. We folded as a coalition and, upon request, passed over the $12,000 in our account to the Fisheries Group, which would sustain for the next four or five years the work we were all trying to do.

Sometime in 1994 or 1995, while I was still in office, one August morning the mailman delivered a letter from a very disturbed parishioner. He was terminally ill with cancer and desperately in need of pastoral care. In spite of repeated requests for a pastoral visit, it seemed to him that he had been overlooked and left out. Now in desperation, his wife advised him to write to me. That afternoon I left the office early and went out to visit him and his wife. When I approached him in the hallway of his home, he said, "I'm a lost sheep, Bishop."

I said, "No, I don't think you are a lost sheep. You are obviously searching for God in your life, for meaning and purpose, and your place in the church."

We sat and talked for the longest while. His story was that he had been baptized as a child and had been in church only once since then that he could remember. One Christmas Eve, when his wife was ready to go to midnight Holy Communion, he came downstairs all dressed up. To her question, "Now, where are you going tonight?" he replied, "I'm going to church with you." In church he felt so uncomfortable and out of place, everything was unfamiliar, and, to add to that, no one spoke to him to make him feel welcome. He stayed only because his wife kept assuring him that it was all right. He never went back to church again.

Now, terminally ill, he was full of questions. Baptism. Confirmation. What is all that about? He very much wanted now to be able to receive Holy Communion. It was a long visit as I tried to assure him and answer some of his questions. In time the rector of the parish and I prepared him for confirmation, sometimes at home and sometimes in the hospital. Then, one Wednesday evening in Lent, I went out for his confirmation and for Holy Communion. The congregation consisted of his family and a few friends. It was a moving service. He couldn't come up to the chancel step and kneel; I had to go down to where he was sitting for the laying on of hands. He was able to come to the communion rail and stand to receive Holy Communion. After the service, while a few photographs were being taken, he came up to me, put his arms around me, and said, "What would I do without God? Now I know where I belong. Now I know my place. I feel accepted, loved, and included."

After that he did get out to church sometimes, particularly in the evening, when fewer people were present and the service was not so long. The rector took him Holy Communion at home as needed. He died some months later and I was given the privilege to preach his funeral homily. I think of him often.

For the longest time afterwards and still today, when I look out over a congregation I wonder if there are people present who feel uncomfortable and out of place. If there are, then we have an additional job to do. The thought is often in my mind. We don't know everyone's life and church experiences or what might be holding them back from greater involvement in the church. When we look into it, the answers are often found in the realm of acceptance, love, and care—pastoral care.

Upon reflection of my leadership style, I conclude that leaders must never cease to be learners. What authority I had was very much a shared authority among synods, myself, the diocesan clergy, and people throughout the diocese. I think my style of leadership was not hierarchical, not pronouncing hard and fast rules, but I hope a sharing and encouraging kind of leadership, personal and pastoral rather than formal. Ministry for me has always been a matter of service—serving God through serving God's people. I tried to enable and encourage people to think for themselves on the basis of the Gospel we proclaim and the faith we practice, all supported by prayer. I have always tried to support people in whatever circumstance, high or low, rich or poor, self-sufficient or very needy. Perhaps because of my background, I seem to identify more with the needy.

With my love of people, my passion for pastoral ministry, and my vision for smaller parishes so that our people could be better cared for, I see myself as an enabler, or as one through whom these people can support the ministry and mission they really want to support. As a priest, and as a bishop, my passion has always been pastoral care. My moments of greatest satisfaction have been when I knew that I had been of service, in Christ's name, to a family, an individual, or a group.

Our home, 13 Cobb Lane, Corner Book, 1978–1997

My installation as metropolitan of the Ecclesiastical Province of Canada at the Cathedral of St. John the Evangelist, Corner Brook, December 7, 1990. Premier Clyde Wells at the microphone.

Stewart as metropolitan of the Ecclesiastical Province of Canada (1990–1997) holding the Metropolitan Cross

Picture taken at the time of my installation as metropolitan in the Cathedral of St. John the Evangelist, Corner Brook. December 7, 1990

One of many baptisms I performed during the course of my ministry.

Confirmation in Deer Lake, Deer Lake parish, at St. Michael's and All Angels Church

Stewart at Killdevil. Killdevil Mountains across the bay in the background.

Stewart, involved in a skit at Killdevil

Stewart in the Killdevil Chapel at a celebration of the Holy Eucharist

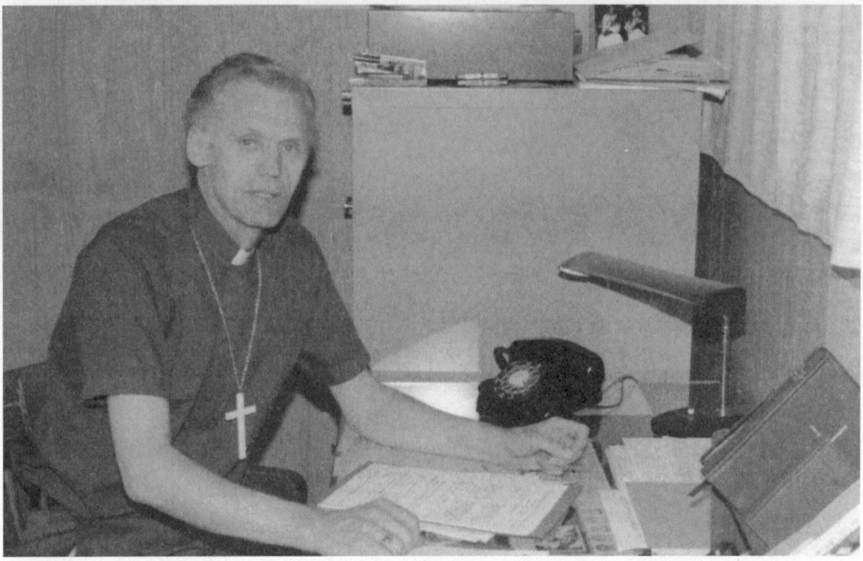

Stewart in his office in the Millbrook Mall, Corner Brook

CHAPTER SEVENTEEN
MINISTRY ABROAD

A few things stand out in my memory of attending the Lambeth conferences of 1978, 1988, and 1998.

In 1978, we were very sensitive to and caring for the twenty-five bishops from Uganda, who were deeply affected by the martyrdom of their beloved Archbishop Janani Luwum the year before. For the longest time they didn't know if Idi Amin would allow them to attend the conference. Finally they were all given passage on a government plane along with a secret police escort. Under surveillance by the police throughout the conference, they were cautious as to when they spoke and what they said. The rest of the conference took care not to question them and to make sure that discussions and resolutions were such as not to adversely affect them when they returned home.

At the 1988 Lambeth Conference, we marked Nagasaki and Hiroshima Day. The war against Japan had ended with the dropping of two atomic bombs, one on Nagasaki and one on Hiroshima, causing devastating suffering to the Japanese people. That evening, at the conference, it was a sombre assembly as we gathered for a service of Light and the planting of a cherry tree near the senate building of the University of Kent. The Primate of Nipon Sei Ko Kai (the Japanese Anglican Church), the Most Reverend Christopher Kikawada, officiated.

At the 1998 Lambeth Conference, Jean Vanier of L'Arche Community conducted a quiet retreat in the form of an all-night vigil which included the washing of feet. Jesus, in washing the disciples' feet, taught them and us the meaning of community, forgiveness, loving service, and oneness. The feet washing under Jean Vanier's leadership reminded us, too, that the church is not about power. It is not that one knows more than the other or that one culture is better than the other, but we are one in faith, servants one of another, each one so much to give, and so much to receive.

The three Lambeth conferences that I attended inspired and affirmed me in the promises I had made at my ordination as bishop in 1978, among them, "to encourage and support all baptized people in their gifts and ministries, to guard the faith, unity, and discipline of the church, and to be merciful to all, showing compassion to the poor and strangers, and defending those who have no help." Those conferences demonstrated to me that people can have different opinions and beliefs, even agree to disagree, but remain in communion, at unity, and as good friends. It is not what I learned from the Lambeth conferences that is most important, but what I have become as a result of those meetings and the bond of love it has strengthened in me, for God and all people.

In 1987, I was asked by the National Church Partners In Mission committee to represent our Canadian Church at the Partners In Mission (PIM) Consultation in Modderport, Diocese of Bloemfontein, South Africa.

Overseas partners were expected to be in South Africa by October 23 and spend a week each in two different dioceses, living among the people, listening to them, and seeing first-hand what were the issues facing the church in South Africa, all in preparation for the Consultation in Modderport in November, which would address a number of issues and make recommendations around justice and reconciliation, a pastoral plan for the renewal of the local church, and the plight of young people in South Africa.

In preparation for the visit I learned that apartheid in South Africa was legislated by the Group Areas Act, 1948. Urban blacks, coloured, Indians, and whites, already segregated to some degree, were all compelled to live in their "own" areas, as designated by the state. Apartheid had been achieved and sustained by law and force, creating untold oppression, hardship, and misery. I also learned that on the outskirts of Johannesburg there was a black township called Soweto, designated to accommodate 800,000 people, but in actual fact the population now was near 2,000,000.

On arrival at the airport in Johannesburg, we were picked up by a white priest from a neighbourhood parish. Because the evening was free, I wanted very much to go out to Soweto, thinking this might be my only chance. For one reason or another it didn't seem possible or appropriate. I got the feeling that some of the white folk kept their distance from Soweto, out of fear. I could understand that because there had been some violent demonstrations and killings in and around Soweto.

The next morning I was up and off to the Northern Transvaal. The plan for me was to spend the first week in the newly inaugurated Diocese of St. Mark the Evangelist, previously part of the Diocese of Pretoria, and the second week in the Diocese of Kimberley and Kuruman.

It was a matter of constant motion in and out of parishes, a day and a night in each community, sharing in many acts of worship, early and late, meeting people and listening to them, sharing who we were and what the PIM conference would be all about.

I spent some time in white areas but most of my time in black areas, and it didn't take long for me to notice the differences between the two. Approaching a white town, so built up and well-kept, one could see on the outskirts or nearby a black township with shabby little houses and none of the modern infrastructure seen in the white community. The white people were marvellous people, too, and had so much more of worldly goods and creaturely comforts compared with what the black people had. In the morning, buses would roll in, filled with black people coming to work as day servants in white homes. At day's end the buses would stop to pick up the same folk and take them back to their own areas. There were some exceptions, no doubt, where black servants were accommodated on property belonging to white people, especially in farming areas. The land designated to black people was always the less fertile and less arable land. Overall, though, the countryside in South Africa is spectacularly beautiful. It was pitiable to see how demeaning the segregation of people can be.

Night after night I had a pretty good idea that I might be the only white person in the black township. As I moved from parish to parish I was so impressed with the genuine, deep commitment of both priests and lay people. They were so friendly, loving, forgiving, and hospitable. The visits were really important because it made them feel that they were not forgotten by the rest of the world and that some changes would come as a result.

The education system in segregated areas left much to be desired. I had the opportunity to visit a school in one black area. It had the bare minimum, with large numbers of children but little by way of teaching aids, resources, and equipment. Yet teachers and children seemed happy and were making the most of what they had.

The church buildings that I saw belonging to the black people were like the schools, just the bare minimum. One such small brick and clay building which I attended had very little by way of church furnishings, a few benches with no backs on them, and a raised chancel area with a very simple altar. In this one case there was no music, yet they sang beautifully, creating a wonderful atmosphere of joy in the worship.

The parishes were very large, one priest serving as many as thirty-six chapelries (congregations) in one parish that I visited. Many chapelries in one parish was not uncommon. We were reminded of the needs of the church to develop God-given gifts and talents, and to train people as Sunday school teachers, youth leaders, lay readers, and as priests. The resources for this work were so inadequate, greatly hindering development and outreach work. It was rare, but I did find, in a few cases, a black priest serving a white congregation, and black and white people meeting together for worship.

I was impressed by the relationship between the clergy and the people. One Sunday morning, this particular black priest and I went off to the eight thirty church service, which was supposed to be followed by the ten o'clock service in another place, some distance away. However, at 9:45, when we left the eight thirty service, he took me back to his house for breakfast, which went on for a while. I became rather anxious and began to show it and finally said, "We don't have much time now to get to the ten o'clock service," to which he replied, "That's all right, they will wait until we get there." Sure enough, when we arrived at the little church, the people were sitting around outside waiting for us. As we went into the little vestry from the outside, they got up and walked into the church, with no questions asked, like, "What kept you?" or "Did you run into some trouble?" The service was truly an inspiration. I said to the priest afterwards, "Where I came from, if you were late like that they wouldn't wait around for you and they probably would not turn up at all the next Sunday."

In the Diocese of Kimberley and Kuruman, the routine was very similar to that in St. Mark's diocese. At a Sunday morning service in the diocesan cathedral, which was a confirmation service, the bishop gave me the distinct privilege and pleasure to lay hands on fifty young people, most of whom were black. I often think about them and wonder where they are now and what they were able to make of their lives. At the Holy Eucharist, while people were receiving Holy Communion, the dean announced that they had run out of wine but that people could continue to receive in one kind. I don't suppose I was the only one whose mind went back to the first miracle that Jesus performed in Cana of Galilee.

The Partners In Mission Consultation, at a retreat centre in Modderport, presided over by Archbishop Desmond Tutu, went well. We all shared our two-week experiences, listened to one another, and made suggestions and resolutions regarding the ongoing work of the church in South Africa.

The highlight of my whole trip happened on the last day before leaving South Africa. At the consultation I met the Reverend David Nkwe, a priest from Soweto. On the last day of my sojourn in South Africa, David picked me up at the synod office in Johannesburg and took me out to Soweto for the day, a dream come true.

Some parts of Soweto may have been better than others, but the path David took led to parts where living conditions were deplorable. The smell from the open sewer by the roadside filled the air. Here and there along the road were water pipes sticking out of the ground, which gave the folk a supply of running water. Women gathered water from those taps and washed clothes right there by the roadside. Housing again left much to be desired. The folks we met and talked to there seemed heavily burdened by the living conditions yet greeted us in a friendly manner and wondered if there was more we could do on their behalf.

We visited the Ipelegeng Community Centre, built in large part by Canadian Anglican Church funds as a centre where people could come for rehabilitation, to learn new skills and trades and grow toward self-sufficiency. David Nkwe took me to a candle-making factory and a sheltered workshop. Finally, we had time only for a brief visit to the Orlando Home for Children, an orphanage started and run by David's wife, Maggie. I still have the book they gave me, called *The Little Sparrows of Soweto*, all about little children who were found abandoned or dropped off at the orphanage. The orphanage was always filled to overflowing because Maggie couldn't turn anyone away. With limited help she cared so lovingly for them all. From Soweto it was a rush to the airport to begin the journey home.

I searched the Internet to find out when apartheid ended in South Africa and found the following information. "In February of 1990, South Africa's President F. W. de Klerk announced Nelson Mandela's release from prison and began the slow dismantling of the apartheid system. In 1992, a whites-only referendum approved the reform system. On April 27, 1994, the first democratic elections were held in South Africa with people of all races being able to vote. The African National Congress won 62.65% of the vote. A Government of National Unity was formed with Nelson Mandela as President and F. W. de Klerk and Thabo Mbeki as deputy Presidents." The many sad effects of the apartheid system will linger for a long time.

Shortly after my trip to South Africa I attended a stewardship meeting in Orlando, Florida. For some reason that eludes me now, at one point we were asked to name an important person or persons we had met in recent time. There was no doubt in my mind that the most important people in my world at the time were David and Maggie

Nkwe in Soweto. I heard a few years afterwards that David Nkwe became a bishop, and I presume that his diocese would have included Soweto.

From November 15 to November 30, 1993, Selma and I were members of a group of twenty-nine from Newfoundland and Labrador visiting Greece and the Holy Lands.

Our group on tour of the Holy Lands, 1993

While in Athens we visited many of the historic sites, like the acropolis of Athens and the Parthenon (Temple of Athena, built between 447 and 432 BC and dedicated to the goddess Athena). We stood on Mars Hill, where St. Paul once stood proclaiming the Gospel to the people. We visited the Olympic Stadium, the birthplace of our modern worldwide Olympics. We did bus tours outside Athens, crossed over the amazing Corinth Canal, visited the acropolis of Corinth and the ruins and excavations in Corinth. Similarly, we took in the acropolis of Mycenea and the surrounding ruins. We spent the better part of a day on the Greek cruise ship *Hermes* visiting several communities on the Greek islands.

On one of the islands we visited a Greek Orthodox church, which some women of the congregation were decorating for a special event. We also visited a nearby fish market before going into a restaurant for something to eat. Language was a bit of a barrier when it came to ordering from the menu. John Davis asked for a plate of fries and was handed a plate of little fish well-fried.

On Sunday morning, November 21, we made our way to worship at St. Paul's Anglican Church in Athens. Nearby was a Greek Orthodox church, and while waiting for the service to start at St. Paul's, some of us dropped in for a few minutes with the Greek Orthodox folk.

Our flight from Athens to Tel Aviv, on Olympic Airlines flight 301, was a night flight. Out over the Mediterranean Sea, we suddenly felt the plane making a very sharp descent. The pilot immediately informed us that he had just received word that there could be a bomb on the plane. When he informed us a second time that there could be a bomb on the plane, he also informed us that we were landing at Paphos on the Island of Cyprus, that we should disembark as quickly as possible, and leave all our personal belongings behind. Apart from a few sobs, nobody panicked. There was absolute silence. We were stunned, deep in thought, processing all the possibilities of the moment. In short order we were on the ground. Buses came out to take us in to the airport terminal.

Going from the plane to the bus to the terminal, several people were in tears and wanted to go home, asking, "Why did we ever come on this trip?" There was no way back, we just had to press on. While I kept assuring them that this was just a scare and that everything was going to be all right, an elderly lady who was deaf came up to me and said, "I didn't understand the pilot very well. I thought he said there was a bum on the plane." Even in the midst of a scary time, you have to be able to see the funny side. We were put up in a hotel for the rest of the night and resumed our journey to Tel Aviv the next morning. We never did find out if there was a bomb on that plane. In Tel Aviv the next day, our story was carried in the local paper, underneath which was the story of a smaller plane that had been brought down by a bomb that same evening, with loss of life.

In Tel Aviv, our tour bus driver and guide met us and we were soon on our way to Caesarea, and then north to Nazareth, the Sea of Galilee area, Capernaum, and some historic sites in between.

In the region of Galilee we stayed in a kibbutz guest hotel. The term "kibbutz" is derived from a Hebrew word meaning "group." The kibbutz is a communal settlement governed by the general assembly of its members. All property is jointly owned, and work, whether agricultural, industrial, or otherwise, is organized on that basis. Members receive no salary but, in return for their work, get housing, clothing, food, medical services, education for their children, and other social amenities.

One of the highlights of the tour for me was to look out over the Sea of Galilee in the early morning, as the sun appeared over the hills on the opposite side, and watch fishermen cast their nets and haul in fish. It was awesome to walk along the seashore where Jesus walked so long ago. One day we boarded a boat and went out on the Sea of Galilee, shut off the motor, and as the boat drifted we read again from the Gospels some of the things that Jesus said and did as He ministered to people with His disciples in that area. Later that same day we celebrated the Holy Eucharist on the lakeshore, on the spot where Jesus prepared breakfast for His disciples as they returned from fishing and said to Peter three times, "Do you love me? Do you love me? Do you love me? Feed my sheep; feed my lambs."

As our group was getting ready for the outdoor service, a Roman Catholic priest from the nearby friary came over to me with a beautiful Eucharistic stole in his hand, and offering it to me he said, "This is a stole the Pope left here for our use. We would like you to wear it as you celebrate the Eucharist for your people." I thanked him very much and wore the stole as we joined in the open-air Holy Eucharist service in that very special place.

In Jerusalem we stayed at Mount Zion Hotel, but we spent almost every waking moment seeing the city outside. First, to get our bearings, we were taken to see a model of the city, including a model of the Jewish Temple. We spent some time at the wailing wall, part of the foundation wall of the Temple which was destroyed about 70

CE, and in the two magnificent mosques on Mount Moriah, where the temple once stood. One was known as the Dome of the Rock. We had the opportunity to do the Palm Sunday walk down the Mount of Olives to the Garden of Gethsemane.

We began one of the days with a visit to the Holocaust Museum in Jerusalem. In the dimly lit museum we walked in eerie silence as we saw the pictures and heard the names of men, women, and children who suffered terribly and died in concentration camps. It set the tone of that day and many more days to follow.

Our last full day in Jerusalem was a Sunday. I had the privilege and joy of preaching at St. George's Anglican Cathedral that day. In the back of this book I will share with you a part of the text of my sermon, in the hope that it captures something of our excitement, gratitude, and awe at being in the Holy Lands.

With hearts bursting with pride, joy, and deep gratitude, early Monday morning, November 29, we took our departure from the Holy Lands, as we made our way to Tel Aviv, Ben Gurion Airport, for Olympic Airways flight 441 to Athens, on our long journey home. Several reunions have been held bringing together all the folks who went to the Holy Lands at that time.

The primate of the Anglican Church of Canada in 1996, Archbishop Michael Peers, gave me the distinct privilege and pleasure to represent him at the ordination of Terry Brown, May 26, 1996, as bishop of the Diocese of Malaita, in the Solomon Islands, in the South Pacific. Terry had been a staff person in our national office in Toronto. The journey covered a twelve-day period.

After a day-long stop in Australia, our flight continued on to Honiara, the national capital of the Solomon Islands, located on the Island of Guadalcanal. From there, in a small twin-engine plane, I flew with others to Auki, where Terry lived in Malaita Province. The church ship *Southern Cross* came a day or so later, having collected, en route, most of the bishops from dioceses in the Solomon Islands, and others who would be attending Terry's ordination.

The ordination service was held in the open air, just outside the small cathedral, and surrounded by beautiful lofty trees. The Most

Reverend Ellison Pogo, metropolitan archbishop of Melanesia and bishop of Central Melanesia, presided. A very large number of people attended, many walking from far away and some riding in the back of pickup trucks. The service lasted a long time; no one was in a hurry. Following the beautiful service, we all shared in a traditional feast, also in the outdoors.

Stewart and Bishop Terry Brown at Terry's ordination on May 26, 1996, as bishop of the Diocese of Malaita in the Solomon Islands

For the traditional meal they used large barbeque pits in the ground, which were fired up and left smouldering throughout the night. Here the meat was wrapped in tinfoil and barbequed. Served with a number of delicious salads, it was nothing short of a feast. Some of the dignitaries sat at tables, but most of the people sat around on the grass and joined in.

I was most impressed by the Melanesian Brotherhood, a large group of Melanesian males who train and commit some years of their lives to the work of the Gospel in those parts. They performed beautifully in traditional chant and liturgical dance, during the service and after. One of the things they do in support of their work and themselves is to craft and sell beautiful Crosses from different kinds of shells. The pectoral Cross I have worn ever since then was a gift from the Melanesian Brotherhood. The Cross is made of tortoise shell, with symbols of the bishop's mitre—a hat in the shape of tongues of fire, symbolic of the Holy Spirit—staff, a chalice and paten, and loaves and fishes, all inlaid with mother-of-pearl.

On our return to Honiara I stayed at the Iron Bottom Hotel, so called because of the large number of iron ships sunk in wartime and lying on the bottom of the ocean just offshore. During the next couple of days I visited with John Vandenberg, a staff person from our national church office in Toronto, several of the development projects supported in part by the Primate's World Relief and Development Fund (PWRDF). As the official relief and development agency of the Anglican Church of Canada, PWRDF is our response to international development, refugees, disaster, and global justice.

I went down on the waterfront and made contact with a few fishermen who had just returned with their catch. Out on the horizon there was one large factory ship, and the fishermen expressed concern about foreign overfishing and what it could mean for them in the future. I could identify with them totally and shared with them our situation in Newfoundland, Canada, where a moratorium had been imposed on the cod fishery in 1992 because of foreign and local overfishing.

I dropped in at a school, chatted with some of the staff members and children, and saw some of the great work being done in that special school. I spent some time in the Anglican cathedral, a fairly large church building without walls. There are pillars keeping up the roof, but no walls at all. Since walls separate people, keep some in and some out, a church without walls, I thought, what a great concept! Their winters are very different from ours, though.

I was fortunate, too, to be able to visit the Bishop Patteson Theological College (Kohimarama) in Honiara and chat with the Canadian provost, staff, and some of the students. Bishop Patteson was the first missionary bishop in the area and, through some misunderstanding, was killed by native folk. The final gathering I was able to attend was a barbeque at the home of Archbishop and Mrs. Ellison Pogo in Honiara.

It was a tremendous experience all round. The world is a small place. What a blessing to be able to meet and share with brothers and sisters in the faith in a different country and culture from our own. Gratitude abounds.

Underlying our ministry through the PWRDF is that we are all givers and we are all receivers. We operate in a partnership. The need for justice is at the very heart of our concern. We all give and receive in different ways other than through the giving of money, although the giving of money is important, too. We need to be on the ground with our overseas partners, get to know each other, and see the work that our money supports. Just to send a cheque to people overseas and leave it at that is not enough. We go to them, and they come to us. We all share of ourselves the greatest gift of all.

Our overseas partners spend time in Canada and attend meetings of PWRDF. National staff personnel make periodic visits to places where PWRDF has a presence, and visit people and the projects PWRDF is supporting. When funds allow, a member of the PWRDF National Committee is chosen to accompany the staff person on the trip.

As a member of the PWRDF National Committee in 1997, I was given the opportunity to accompany the national staff person, John Vandenberg, on a visit to the Philippines in May of 1997. Arriving at the national capital, Manila, we were warmly met and welcomed by representatives of the various agencies in the Philippine Episcopal Church and the Philippine Independent Church that the PWRDF works with in the Philippines.

The next day was a day of rest and orientation. In the morning, we were taken on a courtesy call to the prime bishop of the Episcopal Church in the Philippines, Bishop Saliba. The afternoon was spent in touring Manila and in orientation for the work ahead.

In the course of ten days we covered a lot of territory in and around Manila, Davao City, and Cebu City, especially. We met with, listened to, and talked with fishermen and their families, farmers and their families, and industrial leaders. We observed the way they lived and the concerns they had. We visited a number of sites where development projects, supported by the PWRDF, were in progress. In every case the folk explained to us the difference the PWRDF was making in their lives, their self-esteem, and confidence.

I was struck by the natural beauty of the Philippines, so rich in natural resources, in the fertility of the land, in the prospects for agriculture and mining, yet so underdeveloped and exploited. The history of the Philippines, like that of many other indigenous peoples, is a history of foreign rule, exploitation, and occupation.

I was struck, too, by the plight of the poor. Running through Manila is the Pagas River. In one location, at Peola, on the bank of the river, were some 20,000 families who had come in to Manila from Mindinao, and the Visayas, seeking their fortune in the big city but now living in abject poverty. We mingled and talked with some of the people there and visited with a lovely couple, Alberto and Sonia, and their children.

One afternoon as we were travelling by car back to our quarters via the Smokey Mountain, we came upon a large garbage dump, a waste disposal site by the side of the road. We pulled to one side and stopped, got out of the car, and took a few pictures to document that what we saw was real. We saw makeshift shelters here and there and people living in the midst of the garbage. A few people were moving among the garbage looking for food and any other thing that they could use. I was deeply moved. We were told that there were people in that dump who would spend their whole lives there, born and grew up there, knowing no other kind of existence. For the longest time I couldn't get that picture out of my mind. It haunts me now when I think about it. One positive bit of information was that from a parish nearby a young woman priest was ministering to those people. Hopefully the situation has been corrected and the people restored to normal community living.

Wherever we went in the Philippines I was struck by the friendliness and warmth of all the people. The importance of family was so evident and the place of religion in their lives took top priority. I still have contact through an occasional email from Bishop Felixberto Calang, a bishop of the Philippine Independent Church, one of the many people I met while in the Philippines.

The little church I attended in the Diocese of St. Mark the Evangelist while in South Africa for the PIM consultation at Modderport, Diocese of Bloemfontein, November 9–13, 1987

The Ipelegeng Community Centre in Soweto, 1987

South Africa worship in a small church

Picture of a dwelling we took along the way in South Africa, during our stay for the PIM Consultation in Modderport, Diocese of Bloemfontein, November 9–13, 1987

Rondoval, type of house used by some of the black people. South Africa, PIM Consultation, October 23–November 13, 1987.

Some women carrying bundles on their heads. We happened to see them as we drove along. We stopped and asked if we could take a picture. During the PIM Consultation, 1987.

The ordination of Bishop Felixberto Colang in the Philippine Independent Church

Living quarters for some of the people in the Peola location on the Pagas River, running through Manila

CHAPTER EIGHTEEN
RETIREMENT ON THE HUMBER

Throughout 1997, all my parish visits were, in a sense, farewell events. I had advised the parishes beforehand that if there were to be any farewell gifts they should be monetary in form and given to Queen's College. My last diocesan synod was in Ramea, April 1997. The theme of the synod was "Celebrating Christ in time of change." We gave some time and thought to plans and preparations for the electoral synod coming up in June in Corner Brook to elect my successor. It was during a session in St. Boniface Church, in Ramea, dealing with plans for the June synod that, one of the youth delegates, Chris Warren, in a brief presentation spoke of the "new bishop" and inadvertently referred to me as the "old bishop." The synod exploded in laughter, to the speaker's astonishment.

As the time for retirement drew near, Selma and I had to decide where we would like to live and the things we would like to do in retirement. We had spent the last twenty years in Corner Brook and felt no desire to move out of the area. Whenever I saw property for sale in or near Corner Brook, I wondered if this might be a spot for retirement. In the meantime, I had bought a piece of land in the community of Meadows on the north shore of the Bay of Islands, thinking that we would build a retirement home there.

Canon Thomas Moulton and I were driving through Little Rapids, just outside Corner Brook one day, and saw a sign that said, "Land for Sale." I knew that our daughter Carla was planning to build in Little

Rapids, so we stopped at the house and inquired of the size and price of the building lots. We thanked the lady of the house and walked back to the car. In the process I said to Tom, "I wouldn't like to live in Little Rapids; it's too inland. I would want to see the water, something like where I grew up."

One day when I came home from meetings abroad, Selma informed me that there was a house for sale in Little Rapids, not far from where Carla intended to build. We went out to look at the house, only to discover that it was the same house where Tom and I had stopped to inquire of building lots. Selma thought it was a good spot for retirement, so we made the decision and proceeded to buy the property. We didn't do much with it at first, but in late 1996 and early 1997 we carried out a lot of renovations. Christopher, Robert, and some of their friends went to work on the inside and stripped it bare in some places. I then engaged carpenters to make the necessary changes and to refurbish the place. The electrical service was replaced, as well as some of the wiring. We removed the old dilapidated sun porch on the back side and added a new one with lots of large windows all around. A couple of months before retiring, in August of 1997, Selma and I moved in, so that the Bishop's Residence in Corner Brook could be made ready for the new bishop who would succeed me.

Meanwhile, I sold the piece of land in Meadows. A couple of years into retirement we put a new roof on the house, replaced the kitchen cabinets, and built a detached garage. The sun porch became the main feature of the house. How Selma loved to take her tea and sit out in the sun porch! I enjoyed it, too. Whatever the weather was like, in summer or in winter, it was great to sit there in comfort, read, watch the news, enjoy the scenery, and observe what was going on outside. It was also a great place where I could sometimes stretch out and have a snooze.

In the November 1997 issue of the *Newfoundland Churchman*, I wrote, in part, the following: "Coming to retirement on October 31, I look back with thanksgiving over forty years of ordained ministry in the Church; forty years a priest, nearly twenty of those years as a bishop and seven of those years as an archbishop. I thank God for the call, for the opportunity and privilege of service in many areas and many ways. On behalf of Selma, our four children, Carla, Chris, Robert, and Angela, and our chosen daughter Veronica, may I say 'Thank you' to you all for your acceptance, love, co-operation and support over those years. Our gratitude abounds to the people in my home parish of Fogo, the people in the parishes of Lake Melville (my first Mission of Happy Valley, Mud Lake, North West River and Rigolet is now called the Parish of Lake Melville), Bay Roberts, and St. Anthony, the people of the Diocese of Western Newfoundland, the Ecclesiastical Province of Canada and the Anglican Church of Canada. There are so many names that come to mind but it is dangerous to mention some names and not others. In retirement our relationships will still be there but they will be somewhat different. As long as we have health and strength we will serve the Lord in gratitude and love for all His blessings. Thank you to all of you again. May God's grace and love abound to His praise and honour. Your friend, Archbishop Stewart."

Our Diocese of Western Newfoundland hosted a retirement dinner in grand style at the Pepsi Centre. Again there were many expressions of gratitude and well-wishes for a long and happy retirement. On Sunday, October 19, we met at the Pepsi Centre for worship.

The actual retirement date, October 31, 1997, arrived. There was a feeling of sadness that comes naturally at the conclusion of any endeavour. Coupled with the sadness was a feeling of accomplishment in several areas of diocesan work and humble satisfaction in active ministry as a bishop for nearly twenty years, executed to the best of my ability and with God's continuous help. I hasten to remind others and myself that you retire from the office, from the position, but you never retire from ministry as service to others.

It was difficult to anticipate taking leave of the office and the office staff—Jerry, Rickie, Brenda, and Gordon—for the final time. We had worked together for a long time as a team. A better and a more supportive staff I could not wish to find. But the time had come. We hugged and said farewell for now, but we'd keep in touch. I had kept in touch with Jean Clarke, who had been in the office with me as office manager, secretary treasurer, and my secretary for eighteen years. Jean passed away December 23, 2012. At the time of her retirement around 1995, I wrote a poem in Jean's honour. To honour her now, here are just two verses from that poem.

Always cheery and informed
She managed the office well
As secretary, treasurer, registrar
The atmosphere was swell

Jean and I became a team
Right from the very start
She was as much devoted to her work
As she was to her husband Art.

We stayed on as parishioners at the Cathedral of St. John the Evangelist in Corner Brook, where Selma was involved with the Anglican Church Women and had been a member of the cathedral choir ever since our coming to Corner Brook in 1978. Most of what I did and continue to do as an honorary assistant at the cathedral is home communion for the elderly, sick, and shut in, and fill in whenever and however needed. In the meantime, Selma and I went down to Stonington, Massachusetts, on two separate occasions for two to three months each time, to fill in for the rector of Calvary Church, the Reverend Mark Robinson, while he was on sabbatical. Mark had been a student minister in Western Newfoundland prior to his final years of theological study and ordination. From Little Rapids I filled in at the cathedral in Corner Brook for two months prior to Dean Michael and Hiliary Rice's arrival. From Little Rapids I also helped out, part-time, in Deer Lake parish for a few months, prior to the arrival of the Reverend John and Kelley Meade.

Ever since the beginning of retirement I have been a mentor in the "Education For Ministry (EFM)" program, which is a four-year lay ministry training program. EFM helps us identify our gifts and see how they are being used in service to others. The participants and mentor attend a two-and-a-half-hour seminar every week from September to May each year, thirty-six seminars in all.

Jean Clarke, my office manager and secretary for eighteen years

Synod office staff at the time of my retirement in 1997. Left to right: Brenda Hurley, Archbishop Stewart Payne, Archdeacon Jerry Colbourne, Ricki Murley, and Gordon Billard.

Our home in Little Rapids, 1997–2009

Tomatoes in the garden at Little Rapids

Our property in Little Rapids held great potential for me, because I love the outdoors and gardening especially. I made two nice gardens on the property, had a pumpkin patch, black currants, raspberry vines, and a rhubarb patch. I grew lots of tomatoes, potatoes, beets, carrots, parsnips, and Swiss chard. The joy of harvest time was having plenty to share with neighbours and friends and having a pumpkin for each of the grandchildren at Halloween. It was an especially exciting time for me when I could invite the grandchildren to come at a certain time and choose their pumpkin for Halloween.

After a few years preparing the soil by hand, the children thought the work was getting to be too hard for me and that I should get a rotor tiller. I gave in to the idea and went off to Canadian Tire one Saturday morning to see what they might have by way of a good gardening machine. In the parking lot of Canadian Tire I met Sterling Randell. We chatted for a while, he told me what he was doing, and I told him that I was looking to see what I could find at Canadian Tire by way of a rotor tiller.

There wasn't a heavy-duty tiller to be had at Canadian Tire that day. When I arrived home in Little Rapids there was a message from Sterling, telling me to hold off on a tiller because he knew where I could get one, but I would have to wait until Monday. I was pleased and excited, thinking that Sterling might direct me to a good second-hand tiller somewhere in the area.

Sunday morning would mark the fiftieth anniversary of my ordination as a deacon. Selma and I went off to the Cathedral Church. After the service we went downstairs for the fellowship, coffee time. I was in the upper end of the parish hall, chatting with folk and drinking my tea, when Dean Rice called order and invited me to come to the far side of the hall. There, sitting in the middle of the floor, was a brand new heavy-duty tiller. Dean Rice, on behalf of the parish, presented me the tiller as a fiftieth anniversary gift. It was unreal. I didn't deserve anything like this. When I caught my breath I tried as best I could to say how very, very thankful I was. For several years I was able to use it and it made gardening much easier.

It was a ritual for several years, sometime in November, to get word from Sidney Morris in Robinsons, Bay St. George, that the kelp was in. That meant they had had the right strong wind and kelp was high on the beach there. Then my friend Foster Lamswood, a retired teacher who had started his teaching career in Happy Valley with me when I was chairman of the Anglican-Moravian school board in Happy Valley, and I would go out to the beaches in Robinsons, fill the pan of the truck with kelp, eat our lunch, make our way back, and spread the kelp on our gardens. It took up most of the day, but it was a great outing. It was all very worthwhile, knowing that kelp is the best fertilizer for the garden.

CHAPTER NINETEEN
SELMA

As we neared retirement in 1997, Selma made the comment to me, "You have travelled enough. Stay at home with me from now on."

I heard her clearly, and continue to stay with her, and enjoy the gift she has always been to me, our children, grandchildren, and all who know and love her.

By the year 2006, it was quite evident that Selma was having real health issues as far as memory was concerned. When the neurologist first examined her, he said he didn't think there was anything sinister. Within the year, while she was once in the hospital in Corner Brook, he saw her again and this time felt that it definitely was a form of dementia. I understand from the neurologist that the term Alzheimer's is used loosely for all kinds of dementia.

Our family physician felt that Selma had vascular dementia. Selma had a heart problem and had had several "weak turns" that could be classified as mini-strokes, the first of which left her with double vision and some difficulty sitting down and getting to her feet. To help with the vision problem, it was necessary to cover, alternately, one of the lenses in her glasses. The inability to sit well and to get to her feet corrected itself after a couple of months, and about the same time one morning when I was working on her glasses, she informed me that she didn't need the lens covered anymore, that she could see perfectly well. God's will is always for our wellness and healing. Healing takes place again and again, not always resulting in a cure.

In 2007, the dementia seemed to progress to the point where I couldn't leave her alone anymore. When I went outside to work in the garden she would watch from the window and call me to come in with her, becoming more and more agitated all the time. Thereafter I had to stay put or take her with me wherever I went. For that period of time, on EFM nights, I would take her along to Corner Brook and leave her at our daughter Angela's house while I did my EFM seminar.

The family was anxious that we move closer to them in Corner Brook and not have the highway to contend with in the winter. In 2008, we built a one-bedroom apartment onto Kenny and Angela's House, 101 East Valley Road, thinking that we would spend the winter months in Corner Brook and return to Little Rapids for the summer months. We moved into our apartment in February of 2009.

In the summer of 2009, Selma and I spent very little time in Little Rapids because I couldn't leave her alone in the house long enough to properly do the gardening. It soon became evident that I would have to employ a personal care attendant for Selma, and that would be difficult to do out in Little Rapids. We needed to be in Corner Brook year-round, where we could better access home care support. Eventually I had to face the reality that, if I couldn't utilize the place in Little Rapids, then I might as well sell it. It was a profoundly sad time, because of Selma's health issues, having to leave such a beautiful country home with gardens, and to have to make all the decisions and do the work related to them alone. Selma had been very much a part of the decision to purchase the property in the beginning and really enjoyed everything about it, but now she didn't even realize what was going on. As we packed up to move she would ask, "What are you doing with that?" and, "Why are you carrying that away?"

Since early in 2009 to August 2013 we had home care support, self-managed, increasing the hours from time to time. In a self-managed home care support program I needed the services of a certified bookkeeper. Jeff Follett and David Hounsell, chartered accountants in Corner Brook, made the services of a bookkeeper in their office available to me. I am most grateful to Jeff and Dave, and Marilyn Cave, the actual bookkeeper. Darlene Hiltz was with us as a personal care attendant for Selma from the very beginning of the self-managed home care support program and has become a close friend of the family. October 11, 2012, marked the fiftieth anniversary of Selma's and my marriage. It was a day filled with mixed emotions. On the one hand I was happy and grateful that we had reached this milestone, but deeply saddened that Selma, because of her dementia, was not even aware of the anniversary or what it was all about.

Selma was admitted to hospital in Corner Brook August 23, 2013, with a urinary tract infection. Her condition deteriorated rapidly to the stage of being completely immobile. I saw this coming, because for months prior to being hospitalized she was fast becoming immobile. To get her to walk I would have to take both her hands and walk backward myself, slowly guiding her steps. She was in the hospital in Corner Brook for eight months with no prospect of coming home. She spent the month of May 2014 in the Bay St. George long-term care facility in Stephenville Crossing, awaiting admission to the long-term care facility in Corner Brook. On June 1, 2014, Selma was transferred to the facility in Corner Brook. The care at both long-term care facilities, Bay St. George and Corner Brook, is very good. As family, we are with her every day, trying to make her room homely, tending to some of her personal needs and feeding her most mealtimes. She has progressed to the point of seemingly having no recognition and no real communication, though one can never be sure of those things.

My ministry, throughout her illness, first and foremost, is to care for Selma. I have a ministry, too, in a number of ways as I respond to obvious needs for love and service, chiefly through the EFM program, assisting at the cathedral, and leading a monthly worship service for seniors at the Mountain View Estates Home in Corner Brook. I volunteer, too, collecting for the Heart and Stroke Foundation in February each year.

For physical exercise, social contact, and pleasure, in 2011 I joined one of the teams in the seniors bowling league with Centre Bowl in Corner Brook. From September to May we bowl every Friday afternoon. I use the bicycle—not all that much—that the children gave me as a seventy-ninth birthday gift, and I endeavour to walk for about an hour every day, depending on circumstances and the weather.

Stewart and Selma at Niagara Falls

Stewart and Selma, on one of our travels to meetings on the mainland

September 1988. Paul, Roy, Selma, Tom, and Clem Penney Sr. "Pop" in front, ninety-one years old.

CHAPTER TWENTY
BACK HOME TO FOGO ISLAND

There is quite a contrast between Fogo Island as I knew it, growing up there from 1932 to 1949, and Fogo Island today. I have gone back to my hometown of Fogo at least once a year since leaving to go to summer school in 1949. The only relatives I have there now are two nieces—Margaret Oake and Janet Gill, and two nephews—Gerald Hart and Bruce Payne, and their families and several cousins. The changes that have taken place, through a slow and not always easy process since 1949, are phenomenal.

Stewart and niece Margaret (Hart) Oake, Fogo. The family's mainstay in Fogo.

By the 1960s, life in the ten separate communities on Fogo Island had come to a crisis situation. The inshore cod fishery, which had brought people to the island in the first place and was the mainstay of the island's economy, had failed. The fish merchants, Earle Sons and Company in Fogo and Barr'd Islands, the Newfoundland and Labrador Export Company in Fogo, and the Fishermen's Union Trading Company in Seldom, had had their day and closed shop. This crisis occurred at the same time in many of our Newfoundland coastal communities.

Government could not provide essential services to all the small communities around our shores. The Liberal Government with Premier Joey Smallwood at the helm introduced a provincial policy of resettlement. On September 27, 1967, he told the people of Fogo Island that they had three options: stay as you are; resettle; or develop. Naturally there were some who felt like staying the course, and others who would opt for resettlement, but the leadership on Fogo Island, with approximately 5,000 residents, were not prepared for anything short of development.

I like this exchange between on official from Ottawa and a Fogo Islander. The official asked what was all the talk about resettlement and what would one do if he were moved. Without giving an answer the Fogo Islander shot back, "What would you do if you was put in a boat?"

"I wouldn't know what to do," the official said.

To that came the response, "That's just like the people on Fogo Island. They wouldn't be able to do nothing if they was moved."

The Fogo Island of my youth described a geographical area, not a community. Over the years, it has evolved. A significant development during 1965 was Dan and Grace Roberts's new motel in the centre of Fogo Island. The motel played a big part in the island's development. It offered accommodations to people from off the island. It afforded a central meeting place for residents in the various communities, to eat out, party, and attend meetings, workshops, and conferences.

The members of the Fogo Island Improvement Committee, individually and collectively, must be given much credit for the parts they played in the island's development during that period. They combined efforts and worked closely with the co-operative in building and paving roads on the island and in getting a car ferry service to the island. A big step forward was made in 2011, when the one municipal town council was formed to include all the communities on the island. Each has its own community identity, but there is a great deal more togetherness and one community spirit.

The education of children on Fogo Island became more of an issue as development proceeded. The educational facilities were long outdated and woefully inadequate, each community with its multi-grade classrooms in separate, small, denominational schools. The provincial government had put in place a Royal Commission on Education and Youth, which produced a number of recommendations. With regard to Fogo Island, the recommendation was that the whole school system be consolidated under one interdenominational school board, with one regional high school and five elementary schools, one in Tilting, Joe Batt's Arm, Fogo, Seldom, and Island Harbour. This would amount to complete consolidation.

An amalgamated school board was put in place in 1968 with representatives from the various communities, and Reverend Ivan Jespersen as chairperson. Ivan was the United Church minister on Fogo Island. He produced a local paper called *Fogo Island Profile* to facilitate communication between the amalgamated board, people in the several communities, and government officials on and off the island, and to share information on the progress being made in the school consolidation. It took five years of steady, hard work, but finally, in September 1972, the Fogo Island central high school opened its doors to 600 students: junior high and high school students in grades seven to eleven, from all the communities on Fogo Island.

A few years later the high school was enlarged and renovated to accommodate not only the junior and high school students, but the elementary students as well: all the students on Fogo Island were under one roof.

Large-scale overfishing for a number of years resulted in the depletion of the cod stocks and the total collapse of the commercial cod fishery. In 1992, the Government of Canada had imposed a moratorium on the fishing for northern cod. The moratorium is still in effect, with a limited food fishery and a three-week commercial cod fishery known as the stewardship fishery, for each of the core fishers each year. The moratorium resulted in unemployment for fisherfolk, fish plant workers, and many others in businesses related to the cod fishery. It meant the closing of fish plants and the idling of fishing boats and fishing gear. For a few years the federal government, which regulated the fishery, gave those affected some compensation in lieu of earnings, popularly known as "the package." Although some were able to sell their fishing licences back to the government and retire, the majority of them, when the package program ended, had to look elsewhere for meaningful employment. The out-migration was huge, to the point of depleting the population in some of our coastal communities. The population on Fogo Island was sadly affected, going from 5,000 people in the 1960s to 2,706 people in 2006. However, the co-operative system remained strong, and the offshore fishery, taking many different species, employing longliners and their crews, continued, as did the processing of fish locally.

Zita Cobb grew up in Joe Batt's Arm on Fogo Island, got educated, did very well in business, and came back home in 2006. She began her efforts to give back to Fogo Island by setting up a scholarship program at the local school. At an awards evening she was approached by a parent whose attitude was that scholarships were all right, but it would mean enabling young people to leave Fogo Island and find their niche elsewhere. Zita realized then that something more had to be done for the total population of Fogo Island and Change Islands, the fishers, the seniors, the gardeners, and the square dancers.

Zita was well aware of the good work done in the 1960s by the Memorial University Extension program and the National Film Board known as the "Fogo Island Process." In 2007, she established the Shorefast Foundation. The foundation takes it name from the mooring that attaches a cod trap to the shore. This is a very good metaphor for the work that she was about to engage in. She naturally became the president and Gordon Slade became the chairperson of the Shorefast Foundation. The foundation is fiscally resourced largely by Zita's own money and smaller grants from the federal and provincial governments. The strategy of the Shorefast Foundation is to build on the past, protect the environmental and cultural heritage of the island, diversify and grow the economy, and ensure employment opportunities. This strategy was to be carried forward by constructing an ultra-environmentally green, high-end inn, establishing an international arts foundation, and financing a micro-loan fund to enable local people to establish businesses that could flourish in conjunction with the Fogo Island Inn and the arts foundation.

I had heard that Zita Cobb was back home on Fogo Island buying up some properties, old houses and churches that were no longer in use. After a while I discovered something of her plan. Several of the thirty properties have been renovated and restored. The houses are attractive abodes for several world-renowned artists and visitors. The old St. John the Evangelist Church in Barr'd Islands–Joe Batt's Arm has been beautifully restored and turned into a multi-purpose building and a performing arts theatre. Later there appeared on the skyline four artists' studios and the Fogo Island Inn. One of the many fine features of the inn is the pilot project by the National Film Board known as the film house and cinema. The inn employs seventy people. The inn attracts tourists of financial means, which in turn stimulates the local economy. All revenues earned at the inn go back into community projects.

The micro-loan fund was established to help the setting up of businesses to interface with the inn and the arts foundation. Loans up to around $25,000 are made available to people who seriously want to grow a worthwhile business in keeping with the strategy of the Shorefast Foundation. The businesses up and running to this time include a boat-building factory, greenhouses, a taxi company, an ice cream shop, a daycare centre, and a gourmet restaurant. Those service-sector businesses ensure more jobs and allow more people to stay on Fogo Island.

People eager to work at the inn, and others eager to start a business, needed training in their chosen fields. Instead of taking them away from their families and off the island for training, as normally would happen, the Shorefast Foundation brought professionals to the island to train the people at home—an added boost to the economy.

When I visited Fogo Island in August of 2014, I again took particular notice of all the activities housed in the centre of the island. There is the one United Church building serving all the United Church people on the island, and one Anglican Church building serving several communities, including Joe Batt's Arm, Barr'd Islands, Shoal Bay, Seldom-Come-By, Stagg Harbour, and Island Harbour. In the centre of the island is one large all-grade school, the RCMP detachment building, an arena, the Health Care Centre, a restaurant and gas bar, several very fine homes comparable to homes anywhere else in Canada, and the town council office.

It is a blessing to visit Fogo Island. "Back home" is not the same place it once was, but it has not been abandoned, as have so many places along the coasts of Newfoundland and Labrador. One can see the obvious progress in many ways.

POSTSCRIPT

The many hours spent in writing has satisfied a personal need to be meaningfully occupied, several hours a day, when the "personal care workers" were in attendance at home with Selma. You will have noticed how, in three or four instances, I took the opportunity to get in touch again, after years of silence, with people who were part of one or other of my stories. It has all been a very therapeutic exercise, keeping me mindful of who I am, where I came from, and the great journey it has been and continues to be. Finally, many, many thanks again, and may you all continue to journey well.

CONCLUDING REFLECTION

The family has a great responsibility for the nurturing, care, and growth of family members, both physical and spiritual. Yet the family is so fragile and vulnerable and in need of affirmation and support. Each individual in each family thrives on being loved and cared for. We have often heard it said that you have to earn respect. That is true, but there is a basic respect already ours, and freely given, as children of God, which demands all the respect that we can give one to another. We do not have the opportunity to choose our skin colour, to whom we are born, when, or where. We come into this world on an equal footing, as it were. Our growth and development depends so much on family circumstances, and the family's ability to provide for the physical, emotional, and spiritual needs.

Families together, in community, hold the key to so much of our growth, development, and well-being. Unfortunately, we are not all equal when it comes to inheritance, fiscal income, and resources, and we get classed accordingly. There are more programs in place today than ever to supply help where such help is needed, but it is the positive attitudes we have about ourselves, one another, and the love and respect we show one another that help most in all-around physical, emotional, and spiritual growth. We have often heard the saying that it takes a whole village or community to raise a child.

In the midst of the outside community there is the community of faith in the church to which we happen to belong. There, being valued and accepted is of vital importance. In the Gospel stories we see again and again how Jesus, in His ministry, valued people, accepted them where they were, and with compassion met their needs, restoring sight, restoring speech, teaching, and feeding the multitudes. He chose twelve of His disciples and sent them out to do likewise. The world is our field for the ministries of acceptance, love, and service, for Jesus tells us (Matthew 25:35–40): "For I was hungry and you gave me food. I was thirsty and you gave me something to drink. I was a stranger and you welcomed me. I was naked and you gave me clothing. I was sick and you took care of me. I was in prison and you visited me . . . Truly, I say to you, just as you did it to one of the least of these who are members of my family, you did it to me."

This kind of friendliness and acceptance is not limited to the ones whom we like and are like us, and who share in our tradition and worship patterns, but played out in everyday living, wherever we find ourselves.

I have permission from the copyright department of Hope Publishing Company to quote this hymn found in the *Common Praise* hymn book by Fred Pratt Green.

The Church of Christ in every age
beset by change but spirit led,
must claim and test its heritage
and keep on rising from the dead.

Across the world, across the street
the victims of injustice cry,
for shelter and for bread to eat
and never live until they die.

Then let the servant Church arise,
a caring Church that longs to be
a partner in Christ's sacrifice,
and clothed in Christ's humanity.

For He alone, whose blood was shed,
can cure the fever in our blood,

and teach us how to share our bread
and feed the starving multitude.

We have no mission but to serve
in full obedience to our Lord,
to care for all without reserve
and spread His liberating word.

APPENDIX A

Here is a sampling of my schedule of events and parish visits for 1992.

JANUARY
4 – 6 St. Anthony Parish & Pistolet Bay Parish – Inaugurations
12 Stephenville, consecration of St. Stephen's Church
15-16 Eastport, meeting with bishops Mate and Marsh
17 Gander, Queen's College Corporation
23-26 Toronto, National Stewardship Committee

FEBRUARY
2 St. Mary's, Corner Brook, Induction of new rector
9 Cathedral, Corner Brook, Parish visit
16 St. Michael's, Corner Brook, Parish visit
20 St. John's, Integrated Education Council
23 Deer Lake, Parish visit

MARCH
1 St. Anthony, Parish visit
1 Pistolet Bay, Parish visit
8 All Saints, Corner Brook, Parish visit
9-13 Toronto, National Executive Council
15 Bay of Islands, Parish visit
18 Gander, Queen's College Corporation

22 Meadows, Parish visit
29 Pasadena, Parish visit

APRIL
5 Seal Cove, Parish visit
12 Bonne Bay South, Parish visit
25-26 Lunenburg, NS, Congregational development event
29 St. John's, Integrated Education Council

MAY
3 Rose Blanche, Parish visit (Diocesan Lay Readers' Sunday)
10 Bonne Bay North, Parish visit
24 Stephenville, Parish visit
26 Gander, Joint Committee of three NL dioceses
27-30 Waterloo, ON, Anglican Fellowship of Prayer
30 Fredericton, NB, Canadian Mothers' Union

JUNE
4-7 St. John, NB, St. Paul's Church 150th Anniversary
13-17 Toronto, National House of Bishops
18-26 Toronto, General Synod
28 White Bay, Parish visit

SEPTEMBER
10-13 Burgeo, Parish visit, Ramea, Parish visit
17-20 Forteau, Diocesan Synod
20 Forteau, Parish visit
25-27 Bay Roberts, NL, Parish Mission

OCTOBER
1-4 Prince Edward Island, Provincial Council
18 Channel, Port aux Basques, Parish visit
21-22 St. John's, NL, Integrated Education Council
25 Flower's Cove, Parish visit

NOVEMBER
1 Port Saunders, Parish visit
8-13 Toronto, National House of Bishops
15 Isle aux Morts, Parish visit
22 Bay St. George, Parish visit
29 Plum Point, Parish visit

DECEMBER
6 Grand Bay, Parish visit
13 Cow Head, Parish visit
20 St. Mary's, Corner Brook, Parish visit

APPENDIX B

This text is part of the sermon I delivered at the Cathedral Church of St. George when I was visiting the Holy Lands in November 1993.

> "I thank Dean Tidy for the invitation and privilege to preach in your beautiful Cathedral Church of St. George in Jerusalem. Your beloved Bishop Samir Kafiti preached in St. James Cathedral, Toronto, at the opening service of our General Synod in Canada, June 1992. He said in part, 'Greetings from Jerusalem, the marvellous City of our Christian Faith, the City of Good Friday, the City of Easter, the City of Pentecost, where the Church was born.' What a precious gift it is to me to be able to return greetings from Canada to your Bishop and to you all, brothers and sisters in the Faith here in Jerusalem, greetings. Those of you who have lived here for some time will find it hard to imagine our awe-inspiring pilgrimage of the past two weeks. We have visited several cities and towns, lingered long in the shepherds' field, worshipped at several sites, the Holy Nativity, the Mount of Transfiguration, the Mount of the Beatitudes, on the Sea of Galilee and explored the Holy City which we know, too, as the City of Good Friday, the City of Easter, the City of Pentecost, and the place where the Church was born. Bishop Samir Kafiti, in his opening address to our General Synod in Canada in 1992, said also, 'This World is still broken and is further fragmented. New barriers, based on ethnic consciousness, on fanaticism, on narrow religious

fundamentalism, coupled with an unclear image of a New Order that is talked about, are all breaking our small village, the world.' He also said, 'I come from a tortured, victimized Middle East that needs healing. We need to receive from Christians this cup of salvation of life.'

"Contrary to how things are shown in the media, we have seen little of the troubles which beset your Land. The nearest we came to it was a bomb scare on our plane from Athens, Greece, to Tel Aviv last Sunday night. We had to make an emergency landing in Paphos, Cyprus, and spend the night there. That was a stark reminder to us of the brokenness and hurt, not only in the Middle East, but in our world. In our part of the world there is brokenness and hurt, too, more than I can tell, individual brokenness, brokenness in families and communities, brokenness in churches, brokenness between First Nations people and people of European descent, to name a few. How we all need, more than anything else, reconciliation and healing. As we enter the Advent Season now, with the message of preparation for the coming of Christ, in our ears and in our hearts, hear again the words of St. Paul in 2 Corinthians 5:17–20, 'If anyone is in Christ, he/she is a new creation. The old has passed away, behold the new has come. All this is from God who through Christ reconciled us to Himself and gave us the ministry of reconciliation.'

"As Christians we are all called to exercise the ministry of reconciliation, always and everywhere, to bring people into right relationship with themselves, with others and with God, for we can't have one without the other."

Stewart Payne was born at home in Fogo, Newfoundland, in 1932, the tenth of eleven children born to Albert and Hilda Mae (Oake) Payne. Upon graduating high school in 1949, he attended Memorial College in St. John's to train to become a teacher. His first teaching job was in a one-room school at Wild Cove, Seldom-Come-By, 1949–1950, and he went on to teach in another one-room school on Indian Islands for the year 1950–1951. Two years after he had graduated from St. Andrew's School in Fogo, he returned to become its principal.

Stewart began performing as a choir member and lay reader for the Anglican Church early in his teaching career. The seed was planted, and in 1952 he returned to St. John's to study theology at Queen's College. In 1956, Bishop J. A. Meaden sent Stewart to Happy Valley–Goose Bay as a student minister. His experiences in Labrador during the summer of 1956 assured him that his future was in pastoral ministry.

He graduated from Queen's College and was ordained as a deacon in 1957 and a priest in 1958. Stewart returned to Happy Valley–Goose Bay and worked as a minister there for eight years, covering the areas of Rigolet, North West River, and Mud Lake. In 1962, Stewart married Selma Carlson Penney of St. Anthony and they started a family in Happy Valley while Stewart continued his work there.

In 1965, Stewart and his young family moved from Labrador to Bay Roberts, Conception Bay, where Stewart took over as the new rector at the parish. He worked there until 1970, when he and his family left to serve in St. Anthony on the Great Northern Peninsula. In 1978, Stewart was ordained as bishop of the Diocese of Western Newfoundland. He and Selma moved to Corner Brook, where he could better perform his new duties.

While living in Corner Brook, Stewart Payne was elected and installed as metropolitan of the Ecclesiastical Province of Canada, and therefore also became archbishop of Western Newfoundland, a position he held from 1990 to 1997, when he retired. Today Stewart makes his home in Corner Brook.

Selma, me, and the children when they are older.

Selma and Stewart with Veronica in Little Rapids.

Surviving siblings. Back row, left to right: Cyril, Lewis, Stewart.
Front row, left to right, Minnie, Mabel, Beatrice.